From Snorkelers to Scuba Divers in the Elementary Science Classroom

To Tessa and Jackson,
May you experience an infinite number of ah-ha moments and use the joy in finding out how the universe works to make this world a better place.
—Dad

To my loving husband Gary,
I thank you for your part in my journey. You are the reason I smile every day. Your confidence and belief in me has made all the difference.
—Ann

From Snorkelers to Scuba Divers in the Elementary Science Classroom

Strategies and Lessons That Move Students Toward Deeper Learning

John Almarode

Ann M. Miller

Foreword by John V. Antonetti

CORWIN
A SAGE Publishing Company

A SAGE Publishing Company

FOR INFORMATION:

Corwin
A SAGE Company
2455 Teller Road
Thousand Oaks, California 91320
(800) 233-9936
www.corwin.com

SAGE Publications Ltd.
1 Oliver's Yard
55 City Road
London, EC1Y 1SP
United Kingdom

SAGE Publications India Pvt. Ltd.
B 1/I 1 Mohan Cooperative Industrial Area
Mathura Road, New Delhi 110 044
India

SAGE Publications Asia-Pacific Pte. Ltd.
3 Church Street
#10-04 Samsung Hub
Singapore 049483

Program Director: Jessica Allan
Associate Editor: Lucas Schleicher
Editorial Assistant: Mia Rodriguez
Production Editor: Amy Schroller
Copy Editor: Michelle Ponce
Typesetter: Hurix Systems Pvt. Ltd.
Proofreader: Dennis W. Webb
Indexer: Amy Murphy
Cover Designer: Scott Van Atta
Marketing Manager: Margaret O'Connor

Copyright © 2018 by Corwin

Printed in the United States of America.

ISBN 978-1-5063-5364-7

This book is printed on acid-free paper.

SUSTAINABLE FORESTRY INITIATIVE
Certified Chain of Custody
Promoting Sustainable Forestry
www.sfiprogram.org
SFI-01268
SFI label applies to text stock

17 18 19 20 21 10 9 8 7 6 5 4 3 2 1

Contents

Foreword

Webster's Dictionary defines science as *the knowledge about or study of the natural world based on facts learned through experiments and observation.* With the words *study, experiments,* and *observation* in the definition, surely the science classroom is an engaging place to be.

For the past sixteen years of my professional life, I have had the great fortune to visit more than 20,000 classrooms across North America looking for the answer to a simple question: What engages learners? These visits have provided me with a rich research laboratory as well as a personal learning journey of joy and discovery.

While the question sounds simple, the answer is rather complex because we don't all share a common definition of engagement. And perhaps a single definition will not suffice. If we recognize that engagement is not a static state of being but a continuum of responses and reactions to the world around us, we can begin to search for an answer to our question. We *engage* by paying attention, we *engage* through making sense, and we *engage* to make meaning. Although these three stages of engagement are different, each of these is necessary to survive and thrive.

We can say that all humans engage first by paying attention to our environment. When we are sitting on a park bench, we take notice of the skateboarder who whizzes past us, but probably return quickly to the novel we are reading. When the classroom door opens and a student returns from the nurse's office, most of her classmates "see" her return, but continue to work on the task before them. This is because the movement stimulus is not about us—it is *around* us.

We have all found ourselves in a crowd at a party (or in a loud classroom) surrounded by multiple conversations that become almost overwhelmingly noisy. Yet we are able to use our "selective attention" to focus on the friend in front of us while blocking out all of the other talking in the room. And then it happens. From across the room, we hear someone use our name in their conversation. Immediately, our cognitive brain abandons our friend to seek out the source—is someone talking about *me*?

And that takes us further into the continuum of engagement. We now want to make sense of the world around us and seek out the voices that spoke of us (or *to* us).

If we want to be more engaged in the world, we manipulate our environment and interact with it. We might push through the crowd and look for friends we know. When we find the person who mentioned our name, we are invited to join that conversation (or we invite ourselves). We make meaning by sharing and comparing our experiences and our thoughts with the people who matter to us, to those who can validate us as well as challenge us.

This is how I first met Dr. John Almarode. No, not at a cocktail party, but at an educational conference. I knew of John's work and reputation, but I had not had the chance to work with him personally. That unfortunate lack of collaboration continued until we were in the final hour of the conference. While the conference planner and host felt certain that our messages were cohesive and complementary, we were actually unaware of the connectivity between our component pieces. I had been asked to present a workshop on cognitive engagement while John was work-shopping teacher clarity and intentional lesson sequencing.

School administrators and teachers had been assigned working groups that would "rotate" through sessions—half were assigned to start the day with John Antonetti while the other half worked with John Almarode. While we assumed there was some connectivity between our work, we were independent contractors. As our groups flipped, John and I were both surprised (and pleased) as the teachers shared exciting connections and insights between the two presentations.

The final event of the conference was a panel discussion. It was the first time John and I had a chance to work together. As participants asked questions, they would direct their inquiries and comments to one of us or both of us. A few participants struggled to remember which John A. was which, not because our names were similar, but because our research and presentations were forming a meaningful overlap for the teachers.

What struck me during the panel discussion was that while my work focused on the engagement of our students (as a result of teachers' powerful lesson design), John Almarode's work focused on the teachers' actions and intentional practice (to produce student learning and engagement). We were coming at the classroom from different ends but with the same goal in mind: powerful learning!

The conference experience presented me with something I've known for a long time, but still get excited to realize again and again: there are many ways to enter the learning process. We can start with strong pedagogy or with a curious learner. Regardless of our entry, we want it all: great teaching and excited learners.

In other words, engagement within the learning process is fluid: It moves back and forth across the continuum, sometimes paying attention, sometimes making sense, recognizing connections and then constructing new meaning. It happens in life and in learning. It happens on the kindergarten carpet. It happened in our closing panel discussion, and it must happen in science education.

In this book, John Almarode and Ann Miller provide a beautiful metaphor for transporting our learners across the sea of engagement in the elementary science classroom. Within the metaphor, the authors synthesize the latest research on best practices in science education into a meaningful *flow* of teacher–student–task interaction. They give us a step-by-step protocol for moving our learners from surface experiences into "the deep" in order to explore and make sense of the world around them. The SOLO Taxonomy presented becomes a perfect road map (or perhaps a *sea lane*) for teachers to use as they harness the natural curiosity within our young learners.

In our research on student engagement, we concluded that teachers spend too much time on lesson planning and not enough time designing the cognitive moment. In other words, we spend most of our energy deciding the sequence of the lesson components, gathering the learning materials, making copies of the graphic organizers, and building the presentation slides without clearly determining the cognitive moment we expect our students to have as the critical learning task.

John and Ann ask us to first consider the cognitive processes and tasks that will ensure learning, despite the great range of experiences our students bring with them into the classroom. They then wrap those cognitive tasks into a teaching sequence that keeps the learner moving and articulating connections and responses.

As we are reading about this process of lesson planning, we experience it as a learner through a series of cognitive tasks. Each chapter focuses on a particular component piece of the teaching protocol, allowing us to hone in on the value and research behind that part of the learning.

To help the reader see both parts and whole, John and Ann write and model in the same style they teach: intentionality + clarity + cognitively engaging tasks. Notice how each chapter models and incorporates the efficient, intentional, classroom protocols even if they are not the explicit focus of that chapter. As they introduce each component piece, readers should complete the entry tasks of connection as well as the other cognitive reflections and activities in order to fully experience the lesson methodology. My personal favorites—in the classroom and in this volume— are the *Do* Now activities at the beginning of each chapter, which trust the learners to make sense in advance of the formalized instruction. They allow us to start at the water's edge before we snorkel or scuba dive into the big ideas.

Additionally, the real examples and student work samples allow the reader to recognize the authentic voices of children in the science classroom and to see learning though the eyes of the student.

Learning is messy. The authors recognize and celebrate this truth while helping teachers develop efficient and effective sequences to bring about optimal learning in elementary science.

If you are looking for strategies for students in science, this book is for you.

If you are looking for a book study to move the practice of your PLC, this book is for you.

If you are looking to get the most learning for your teaching, this book is for you.

If you love science, and you love learning…It's time to dive in! Or just wade in for now.

You'll want to go deeper in a bit!

—John V. Antonetti
Colleagues on Call
Former Director of K–12 Curriculum
Sheridan, AR

Acknowledgments

FROM JOHN ALMARODE

The science classroom has always been a special place for me. As a student, I experienced the most ah-ha moments and joy in finding out how the universe works: to think that the easily observed scientific phenomena that is taken for granted on a daily basis is the result of highly complex interactions, principles, theories, and laws. For example, slight movements in the Earth's crust is responsible for the incredible mountain views all over the world and, at the same time, earthquakes and volcanoes. Or how about the interaction between our sun's energy, the rotation of the Earth, and our atmosphere that produces weather patterns across the globe. These are just two examples of highly complex scientific phenomena that are ultimately responsible for the daily life we experience. For some of us, this includes mountain hikes along nature trails that open up to breathtaking views of four distinct seasons (summer, spring, winter, and fall). For others, this complexity produces droughts, monsoons, hurricanes, volcanoes, or earthquakes. In any case, the ability of Earth's inhabitants to respond to whatever environment they find themselves inhabiting relies on an understanding of these phenomena. For example, water storage and purification, drainage systems, hurricane shelters, advanced technology that monitors volcanic activity, and "earthquake proof" housing represent technologies developed by us to respond to the incredibly diverse nature of our planet. How do individuals think up these technologies and then see them put into action? These individuals know, understand, and are able to do science. As the research has suggested for years, these individuals know, understand, and are able to do science because their lives intersected with individuals that were effective at teaching science. This connection was not lost on me. So, I became a science teacher. As I said before, the science classroom has always been a special place for me.

With this in mind, I can state, without any hesitation, that my ah-ha moments, my joy in finding out how the universe works, and my incredible experiences as a teacher would not be possible without several key individuals. The person that inspired me to become a science teacher was my sixth-grade science teacher, Ms. Cross. Her classroom was magic. Each day we were encouraged and supported in getting into the water, snorkeling, and then scuba diving! Yep, she is the starting point, the epicenter, the ground zero. Ms. Cross is still a strong and positive influence on my life. Oh, and my children call her Grandma Sally. Prior to sixth grade, I had incredible teachers that fostered, nurtured, and sustained my desire to scuba dive in my learning and not settle for snorkeling. From kindergarten on, I had the pleasure of learning from teachers that this very book advocates for in every classroom and school around the globe: Mrs. Howell, Mrs. Kiser, Mrs. Wright, Mrs. Stump, Mrs. McCray, Mrs. Grochmal, Ms. Clouse, Mrs. Coleman, and Ms. Clinedinst. For them, I am eternally grateful.

Now to my students! The greatest honor of my professional life is teaching young learners. Period. During my time in the classroom, I enjoyed this honor over and over again. From the young minds participating in STEM activities at the Shenandoah Valley Regional Governor's School to the future elementary educators that enrolled in my elementary science methods course or my inclusive early childhood science methods course, each individual changed my life. Just by interacting with each of them, I developed a clearer understanding of other people's perspective. Just by hearing their voices in the classroom, I developed a clearer view of the experiences that shaped their learning journey. This, in the end, is to what I would contribute any and all of my success. And to my former students, if you read this, I hope you know that my life is better just because I spent part of it with you.

The contents of this book are not just an academic exercise. I have two young children at home. Tessa and Jackson, who you will meet in this book, are my greatest accomplishments. With that being said, the desire for an enriching and engaging learning environment is personal. Tessa is in kindergarten. I hope, with all my heart, that she will experience learning that will compel her to be a lifelong scuba diver. Jackson, 2 years later, will enter kindergarten. My hope is the same for him. I want to return to the opening paragraph of this acknowledgement. You see, a majority of the world experiences the negative items associated with the complexity of our scientific world. Water scarcity, poverty, and life in risk regions of the globe are more common than any of us want to admit. However, the only way to make the world a better place is to know, understand, and be able to do something with the knowledge of how the world works. The young minds that fill our classrooms today will be the adult minds that, at first, snorkel and then scuba dive into learning and develop the technologies that not only change lives but save lives. Our commitment should be to providing enriched and engaging learning environments that make this happen. I want that for Tessa and Jackson. So, Tessa and Jackson, thanks for putting a personal face on why I do what I do!

And last, but certainly not least, I want to thank my wife, Dani. I am still married after another book project. Her support is amazing. Your unyielding support in each and every endeavor does not go unnoticed. I am grateful you are my wife, and I am even more grateful that we are partners in life. Thank you.

FROM ANN M. MILLER

Most people can easily and quickly identify a life-changing science teacher. My life-changing experiences started many years ago in the finished basement of a ranch home in Smithtown, New York. My science teacher was my dad. Antone Mileska was an electrical engineer by trade, but to me he was a wealth of knowledge who always had the answers to my questions. He knew how to spark my curiosity and stimulate my thinking just enough to trigger a world of exploration. Thanks, Dad, for the strong foundation and wonderful memories. I am eternally grateful.

Today, as I enter our elementary classrooms, I observe teachers eager to stimulate student thinking and tap into their sense of inquisitiveness. A teacher's level of enthusiasm can have a significant impact on both teaching and learning. Did you know that enthusiasm is contagious? It definitely is for me. My love, inspiration, and motivation to learn and grow in the area of science comes from the classrooms I walk into every day. I truly love working and collaborating with these creative and dedicated teachers. For that reason, I want to thank those teachers who have given me the opportunity to grow and learn with them.

Embracing challenges and hard work is not always easy. There are people in our lives that make it look so easy. John Almarode is one of those people. I want to thank him for his continuous encouragement and confidence in me. He truly is an inspiration. I am so glad he reached out and gave me this opportunity. Too many of us fail to see the greatness within ourselves. John, thank you for sharing your innovative thinking while becoming a valuable friend. You gave me the chance to discover my own potential.

To my family who has always inspired me to be me, I say thank you. Thank you for constantly being by my side; your support, prayers, and love will never be forgotten. I only wish I could give back as much as you have given.

PUBLISHER'S ACKNOWLEDGMENTS

Corwin gratefully acknowledges the contributions of the following contributor:

Dr. Jenny Sue Flannagan
Associate Professor
Martinson Center for Mathematics and Science at Regent University
Virginia Beach, VA

About the Authors

Dr. John Almarode has worked with schools, classrooms, and teachers all over the world. John began his career in Augusta County, Virginia, teaching mathematics and science to a wide range of students. Since then, he has presented locally, nationally, and internationally on the application of the science of learning to the classroom, school, and home environments. He has worked with hundreds of school districts and thousands of teachers in countries as far away as Australia, Canada, England, Saudi Arabia, Scotland, South Korea, and Thailand. In addition to his time in PreK–12 schools and classrooms, he is an associate professor in the department of Early, Elementary, and Reading Education and the codirector of James Madison University's Center for STEM Education and Outreach. In 2015, John was named the Sarah Miller Luck Endowed Professor of Education. At James Madison University, he worked with preservice teachers in elementary science methods and actively pursued his research interests including the science of learning and the design and measurement of classroom environments that promote student engagement and learning.

The work of John and his colleagues has been presented to the United States Congress, Virginia Senate, and at the United States Department of Education as well as the Office of Science and Technology Policy at The White House. John has authored multiple articles, reports, book chapters, and two books including *Captivate, Activate, and Invigorate the Student Brain in Science and Math, Grades 6-12* (Corwin, 2013). However, what really sustains John, and his greatest accomplishment, is his family. John lives in Waynsboro, Virginia, with his wife Danielle, a fellow educator, their two children, Tessa and Jackson, and Labrador retrievers, Angel and Forest.

John can be reached at www.johnalmarode.com.

 **Ann M. Miller** has had the privilege of working as an educator and staff developer for many years. She is currently the coordinator of elementary instruction and professional development K-12 for Waynesboro Public Schools. Ann began her career teaching Special Education for Cayuga-Onondaga BOCES in Cayuga County, New York. She focused her efforts on emotionally disturbed students before making a successful transition to the position of instructional specialist. Ann became a member of an elite team of staff development leaders where her enthusiasm, knowledge, and approachable style helped to develop strong productive learning communities within nine different school divisions. Her extensive knowledge about teaching, student engagement, and how children learn has provided a strong instructional foundation needed to design, facilitate, and implement relevant and meaningful learning opportunities for a wide range of audiences. Ann truly loves her career, but she would be the first to tell you how truly blessed she is to have a loving and supportive husband, three caring children, and four terrific grandchildren. Everyone should be so lucky.

Introduction

Read not to contradict and confute; nor to believe and take for granted; nor to find talk and discourse; but to weigh and consider.

—Francis Bacon

Tessa is an inquisitive, extraordinary five-year-old who wants to be a marine biologist when she grows up. Seriously. When asked what she wants to be when she grows up, this quizzical young girl responds without hesitation, "I want to be a marine biologist because I love dolphins." Regular trips to the library result in the checking out of several books about dolphins or whales, many of which are then kept in her room well past their return date. Her curiosity is not limited to dolphins or even aquatic ecosystems and the living and nonliving members of those ecosystems. Her incredible curiosity about everything is palpable.

Tessa asks questions at an incredible rate of speed, rapidly firing inquiries about, say, spiders, bugs, numbers, letters, clouds, or music at anyone within earshot of her. Just recently, she raced outside in the rain to take a long look at an earthworm using its muscles and setae, or tiny bristles, to inch across the driveway. *Why this? Why that? How does this work?* Yes, at times this can be taxing on the patience of adult bystanders especially if they have other objectives in mind, such as Tessa brushing her teeth, getting dressed for preschool, checking out at the grocery store, or getting ready for bed at night. This is beside the point. The point here is that Tessa's questions reflect higher-order thinking and her desire for understanding. Her questions are not her quest to accumulate countless facts about the world that she can then regurgitate on command. She is trying to make meaning from her experiences and develop conceptual understanding.

Tessa is not unlike most five-year-olds with their unbridled curiosity about the world around them. Many of you reading this can think of a specific young learner, whether in your personal life or professional life, that resembles Tessa. Tessa is scuba diving. Thus, you will also note that when there are significant gaps in background knowledge of these young learners, that is, they don't have the prior knowledge to ask why or how, they do ask, what is that? Young learners, like Tessa, know when they need to snorkel. Tessa, and young learners easily and naturally transition back and forth from higher-order questions to questions designed to fill in background knowledge. After all, this is how we learn: moving from snorkeling to scuba diving! Yet, research on today's classrooms paints a picture that is in contradiction to how we learn, and it will have an influence on young learners as they enter the kindergarten classroom. To illustrate this point, take a few moments and select what you believe to be the best answer to the following question:

QUESTION BOX

At what point does research say that children stop asking questions in school?

(a) Elementary School: Kids learn that teachers value right answers more than a provocative question.

(b) High School: Teenagers become absorbed in other matters relevant to their social world, such as a text message, and interpreting what it means.

(c) Never: Curiosity is an innate feature of the brain.

If you selected choice *a*, you are correct. Young learners perceive, quite quickly, that teachers are looking for the right answers (Medina, 2014a). Thus, curiosity as an innate feature of the brain, at least in classroom learning, is extinguished. Researchers have noticed this pattern in classrooms for years. Yair (2000) found that teachers talk between 70 percent to 80 percent of class time, eliminating the opportunity for student questions. As far back as the late 1970s, researchers noticed that specific patterns in teacher-talk lead to low-cognitive learning outcomes (i.e., simply recalling facts). Teachers initiate questions that elicit a student to simply recall facts 60 percent of time, and the teacher evaluates the correctness of the response (Brualdi, 1998; Meehan, 1979). This leads to less time for student-student dialogue and student-teacher discussions (Alexander, 2017; Duschl & Osborne, 2002; Mercer & Littleton, 2007; Newton, Driver, & Osborne, 1999). Again, most of the talking in classrooms is teacher-directed and focused on factual knowledge, giving students 1 second or less to think and respond (Cazden, 2001).

There appears to be no place in the classroom for the questions that reflect higher-ordering thinking and desire for understanding posed by Tessa and other like-minded five-year-olds. Scuba diving is prohibited.

Tessa, and the summary of research on questions and talking in the classroom, highlight just one specific example and situation that is addressed in this book. Each of the following chapters strives to answer one essential question: *How do we foster and nurture student interest and engagement in the K–5 science classroom that promotes higher-order thinking and deep conceptual understanding?* The answering of this question is not without challenges. The age of accountability in education is here, not likely to go away, and will likely gain in strength. Classroom teachers, instructional leaders, and administrators are ever mindful of test scores, other accountability measures, and teacher evaluation systems. Are higher-order thinking and deep conceptual understanding in science possible in today's high-stakes testing environment? This book emphatically argues that yes, this is a possible outcome.

With high-stakes testing and accountability in mind, this book will (1) present an instructional framework that promotes *higher-order thinking and deep conceptual understanding* in the K–5 science classroom that aligns with national- and state-level standards; (2) build an understanding of what science teaching and learning must look like to *engage students behaviorally, emotionally, and cognitively* in K–5 science; and (3) encourage you to *weigh and consider*, as so eloquently stated by Francis Bacon at the beginning of this introduction, your instructional decisions. As part of the bigger picture, the contents of this book will help support schools, classrooms, and teachers as we respond to the recent attention on American students' performance in science relative to the rest of the world and the many initiatives to improve the performance of U.S. students in the learning of science.

Thus, the learning intention of these subsequent chapters is as follows:

> To understand how to foster and nurture learner interest and engagement in K–5 science that results in higher-order thinking and deep conceptual understanding.

This fostering and nurturing must start early. Capturing and maintaining student interest in science leads to more successful learning outcomes for students and greater likelihood of persistence in their science learning. Research has looked at experiences reported by current scientists and graduate students in science disciplines (Maltese & Tai, 2010). *Over 65% of the participants indicated that their interests in science began before their middle school years* (Maltese & Tai, 2010). Furthermore, this early interest was attributed to quality experiences while in elementary school (Maltese & Tai, 2010). The consistent message in the research on interest and persistence in science learning is that early, quality experiences in science lead to earlier interest and the more likely that the student will persist in the learning of science.

The Big Idea

We, as classroom teachers, can provide experiences that foster, nurture, and sustain deep cognitive engagement.

Thus, the instructional framework presented in this book emphasizes the need to foster and nurture student interest in science during the early years of schooling. Within the research, this spark of interest through events similar to an earthworm inching across the driveway is referred to as *diversive curiosity* and often wears off as soon as something new comes along (Leslie, 2014). Thus, *diversive curiosity* alone will not achieve the levels of engagement and persistence necessary for *higher-order thinking and deep conceptual understanding* in the K–5 science classroom.

However, it is a starting point. The instructional framework presented in this book will provide evidence-based practices that promote persistence in science learning or what is referred to as *epistemic curiosity*. Epistemic curiosity, or the deepening of a simple seeking of newness or novelty, is a student-directed attempt to build understanding through sustained cognitive effort (Leslie, 2014). This, in turn, leads to *higher-order thinking and deep conceptual understanding, behavioral, emotional, and cognitive engagement*, and *the greatest impact on student learning* in science.

WHAT TO EXPECT

In the coming pages, not only will this book present an instructional framework, build an understanding of high engagement in K–5 science learning, and encourage you to weigh and consider your instructional decisions, each chapter will model the concepts presented in each chapter. The following in-text features are designed to reinforce each idea and promote the transfer of the information from this book to the classroom:

1. The *metaphor* of snorkelers and scuba divers is the foundation for each chapter, idea, and strategy. This metaphor allows us to link abstract ideas to concrete objects or experiences. This, of course, is how we learn and is required of any future scuba diver.

2. *Learning Intention and Success Criteria* are presented at the start of each chapter. The learning intention is a clear statement about what you should learn as a result of reading the chapter. The success criteria specify what evidence will show whether or not you have met the learning intention.

3. *Do-Nows* are strategically placed throughout each chapter to break up the information into chunks. Each *Do-Now* provides opportunities for you to review, revise, and process information. This, of course, is how we learn and is a necessary part of the learning journey from snorkeling to scuba diving.

4. *Here's How* activities are located throughout the text. The *Here's How* activities provide suggested steps for implementing the ideas and strategies in this book. Keep in mind that each classroom context is unique. *Here's How* activities may need some modifying to work in your specific setting.

5. Closure is important. Exit activities will close out every chapter. Each exit activity is designed to consolidate information from the chapter into big ideas and take-aways. This, of course, is how we learn and will significantly contribute to learners' successful movement from snorkeling to scuba diving.

The in-text features of the book reinforce each idea and the transfer of the ideas by "practicing what we preach." Although the metaphor, learning intention and success criteria, *Do-Nows*, *Here's How*, and exit activities are targeted to you as the learner, each of these features can be modified and used in your K–5 science classroom.

This brings up the final and most important feature of the book: strategies. Each chapter is full of strategies that highlight how to support learners as they move from snorkeler to scuba diver. These strategies are evidence-based practices that can be applied to your classroom as is or be tweaked to better fit your specific classroom context. Furthermore, many of the strategies apply across several ideas. We have worked hard to provide a range of strategies across all levels and science topics in found in a K–5 school.

From Snorkeling to Scuba Diving

In the following chapters, we present the instructional framework that promotes *higher-order thinking and deep conceptual understanding* in the K–5 science classroom that aligns with national- and state-level standards. In other words, this framework fosters and nurtures young learners' learning journey from snorkeling to scuba diving in science. This framework is built from the latest research on how students learn and incorporates examples and strategies that support this journey. Chapter 1 unpacks the snorkeling and scuba diving metaphor. What is a snorkeler? What is a scuba diver? The next chapter explores how learning progresses through surface-level, deep-level, and then deep conceptual understanding. This is the learning progression for our young learners as they snorkel and scuba dive.

Chapters 3 and 4 present the first component of the instructional framework: Young learners must acquire high quality information. Emphasizing a standards-based approach, readers will experience the process of identifying the priority standards in elementary science and how to unpack those standards, readying them for instruction. Using the model developed by Larry Ainsworth (2003, 2010), the chapter will model the process using the Next Generation Science Standards. A particular area of focus for this chapter is that *standards tell us what to teach, not how*. In order to effectively guide students from snorkelers to scuba divers, *teachers must know exactly what to teach so that the how and the what are perfectly aligned*. This requires teachers to build and activate background knowledge.

Chapters 5 and 6 explore the second component of the instructional framework: the use of evidence-based strategies for teaching and learning K–5 science. Once you have determined clearly *what* you and the students are aiming for (i.e., Chapters 3 and 4) you must identify the most appropriate and effective model of instruction and evidence-based strategies. These two chapters will present, discuss, and model various models of instruction by focusing on how *the what* from previous chapters guides and informs the instructional decision, the *how*. Examples of each of the models discussed will be presented through vignettes, highlighting the alignment between the learning intentions, success criteria, and the model of instruction.

Chapter 7 adds the final component of the framework: providing opportunities for young learners to apply their learning to different contexts. What has been suggested in the research on higher-order thinking and transfer is that these are teachable traits or skills. That is, teachers can and do create educational environments that promote *higher-order thinking and deep conceptual understanding* in the K–5 science classroom. This chapter presents this research in a teacher-friendly way, encouraging readers to apply the findings directly to their classrooms. As in the previous chapter, a significant component of this chapter includes an explicit connection between *evidence-based practices* and the unpacked standards, learning intentions, and success criteria from the previous chapters. The difference is that this particular chapter explores the process of *teaching up* with the goal of enhancing the creativity and problem-solving skills of students.

Finally, Chapter 8 pulls it all together by helping you develop an action plan for implementing the ideas from the book. How do you, as a professional, support your own snorkeling to scuba diving journey? So, let's get started. Grab your mask, snorkel, and scuba gear.

EXIT TICKET

What are your goals for reading this book? Before turning another page and moving on to the next chapter, take a moment and create one or two goals you have in reading this book. Please make sure your goal is specific, measurable, attainable, relevant, and can be achieved in a realistic timeframe.

Example: This quarter, I will develop [insert number] strategies or activities that help my students make connections between concepts in science (very specific, measurable, attainable, relevant, and can be achieved in a realist timeframe).

Nonexample: I want all of my students to be engaged (although relevant, very broad, not measurable, may not be attainable on a given day, and there is no timeframe).

Goal #1

_____

_____

_____

Goal #2

_____

_____

_____

Finally, in a sentence or two, write down your vision of success. What will your teaching and the student learning in your classroom look like if you are successful?

_____

_____

_____

_____

_____

_____

CHAPTER 1

What Is a Snorkeler, and What Is a Scuba Diver?

Learning Intention

I understand the differences between a snorkeler and a scuba diver in my classroom.

Success Criteria

By the end of this chapter, the following success criteria will be met:

1. I can compare and contrast surface-level and deep-level learners (snorkelers and scuba divers).

2. I can describe the necessary components in fostering, nurturing, and sustaining deep-level learners.

3. I can apply these components to my own classroom.

As mentioned in the introduction, the ideal outcome articulated by almost all classroom teachers is for their students to obtain higher-order thinking, high levels of engagement, and the transfer of knowledge to other contexts. That is, teachers strive for scuba divers, not snorkelers! So, figuratively and literally, what are snorkelers, and what are scuba divers? To begin this conversation, take a few minutes to complete the first Do-Now. Brainstorm a list of characteristics you believe describe a learner that is figuratively a snorkeler in your classroom. How about a scuba diver?

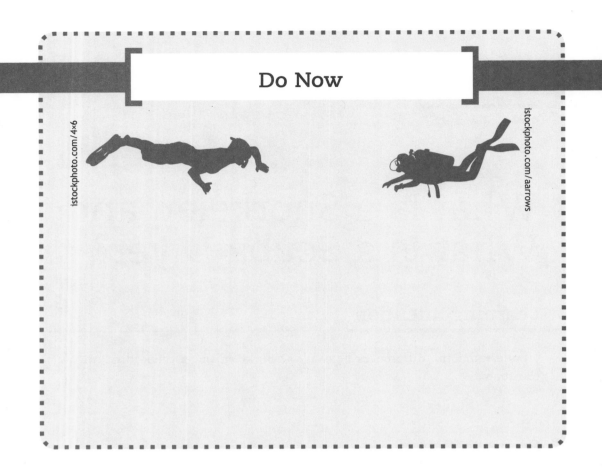

Do Now

A diving friend of mine described his snorkeling experiences as a peaceful feeling of freedom as he moved around on the surface of the water just taking in all of his surroundings. This surface-level exploration provided a safe and relaxing journey of the aquatic ecosystem. On the other hand, the same friend elaborated with great details about safety precautions, equipment needs, the specific location and characteristics of the diving location, and the importance of his diving buddy before going on to talk about the amazing things he observed as he experienced scuba diving off the coast of Roatan, Honduras. The opportunity to deeply engage in the exploration of an ecosystem, getting up close to each and every component of the environment, and unpacking the intricacies and complexities of the underwater world was equally as thrilling to the diver. However, the experience came only after purposeful and intentional preparation for such an amazing experience. And yes, there was more risk involved. The answer to the question, what is a snorkeler, and what is a scuba diver, literally, is easy to extract from the two above described experiences. Figuratively, the two experiences represent the similarities and differences in learners who are snorkeling in your classroom and learners who are scuba diving in your classroom. Let's dive right in and unpack this metaphor so you can be better equipped to set up experiences in your classroom that will move students from snorkelers to scuba divers.

Refer to your responses in *Do-Now* on the previous page. What types of questions and behaviors are you observing in your students?

QUESTIONS	
Why do we have to know this?	Why is that happening?
Is this going to be on the test?	What caused that to occur?
What do I have to do to get this right?	Was that reaction due to _____?
BEHAVIORS	
Completes every assignment	Shows desire to revise work
Recalls facts without elaboration	Asks thought-provoking questions
Compliant with specific directions	Transfer/generalization of knowledge

As you examine the two columns above, how would you describe the differences? Although there are multiple interpretations and images that come to mind, these overall perceptions tap into the idea that every teacher has an assortment of snorkelers (surface/breadth of learning) as well as scuba divers (in-depth/deep level of learning) in their classrooms.

The Big Idea

In our classrooms, there are snorkelers, and there are scuba divers.

Oh, and learners often move between the two depending on the day, time of year, and the specific topic or content.

SNORKELERS VERSUS SCUBA DIVERS

Both scuba diving and snorkeling are great forms of underwater exploration with some basic similarities and very distinct differences. As we examine these two experiences, hold on to the mental representation you create, the opportunities this type of learning has to offer, and focus on the conscious decisions you need to implement within your classroom so students move toward deeper learning. Snorkelers and scuba divers can be defined across three main dimensions:

1. Prior and background knowledge

2. The nature of their thinking

3. The nature of their interactions

PRIOR KNOWLEDGE AND BACKGROUND KNOWLEDGE

Upon initial exposure, it is expected that students will snorkel before they scuba dive. Students in the elementary science classroom must acquire specific content knowledge and process skills necessary for science learning. The surface level knowledge is important and essential in the science learning progression of students.

Content knowledge includes facts, figures, theories, models, and scientific principles. This is the "stuff" within science like, for example, the metric system, life cycles and changes in organisms, the organization of our solar system, or laws of motion. Without this prior knowledge or background knowledge, scuba diving is difficult because, as scuba divers, these students will not have an awareness or appreciation for what they are seeing on the deep dive. They will not be able to identify what is relevant or irrelevant as they move beyond the surface of science content. Of course, what is or is not necessary prior knowledge and background knowledge depends on the content and the grade level. The previous list is just an example to differentiate content knowledge from process skills.

The process skills that make up the prior knowledge and background knowledge include the processes of science: observing; classifying; sequencing; communicating; measuring; predicting; hypothesizing; inferring; using variables in experimentation; interpreting; analyzing and evaluating data; and designing, constructing, and interpreting models. Without this prior knowledge or background knowledge, scuba diving is difficult because as scuba divers, these students will not have the tool kit for actively engaging with what they are seeing on the deep dive. They will not be able to interact with the relevant content as they move beyond the surface of science content.

Snorkelers do not yet have the necessary equipment to scuba dive. Snorkelers lack the prior knowledge and background knowledge to effectively engage in deep-level knowledge and thus regularly cling to surface-level knowledge, preferring to snorkel simply out of necessity. For example, students from disadvantaged backgrounds may not have had the same experiences as their peers and thus do not have the same level of prior knowledge or background knowledge. Similarly, English Language Learners may not yet have the necessary vocabulary to engage in science learning at a deep level. One final example, students with disabilities may need modifications, accommodations, skill building, or enrichment in order to have equal access and opportunity to move beyond snorkeling and engage in successful scuba diving. When these students are asked to scuba dive, they often struggle and, subsequently, behaviorally, emotionally, and cognitively disengage from learning. However, it is worth noting that this struggle is *not due to ability but simply access to necessary content* (Almarode, 2011).

Our role in the classroom is to plan and implement educational experiences, or dives, that represent conscious decisions about how to support learners, regardless of their prior knowledge or background knowledge, as they move toward deeper learning. Just as in real snorkeling and scuba diving, the guide on the boat does not place the pressure of prior knowledge and background knowledge on the shoulders of the divers. Instead, the guide meets the divers where they are and then supports them as they develop their diving skills. This is analogous to the role of the teacher and paramount to the entire learning progression in classrooms.

Snorkelers survey the environment and content in order to determine what to focus on as they move to a deeper level of learning. As a snorkeler moves through the surface of the curriculum, the learner must be given opportunities to form connections, gather additional information, and receive effective feedback in order to make the next dive a more valuable learning experience. When the classroom environment purposefully and intentionally provides these opportunities, snorkelers trade in their snorkel for an oxygen tank. In this case, the oxygen tank is the necessary knowledge and skills to successfully engage in higher-order thinking, engage at high levels, and transfer knowledge to other contexts.

Do Now

When determining which students are ready to exchange their snorkel for an oxygen tank, what characteristics would snorkelers exhibit that would indicate they are ready to scuba dive? On the flip side, what are the warnings signs that students are not ready for the deep water? Take a minute to jot down your thoughts on paper. In doing so, focus on how students' prior and background knowledge influences their ability to scuba dive ∎

The importance of prior knowledge and background knowledge in the learning process is analogous to pressure changes in the diving process. As divers move through different depths in their dive, they experience changes in pressure. Specifically, pressure increases with the depth of the dive. For learners, the pressure to have the necessary prior knowledge and background knowledge increases with the depth of thinking. This poses a risk for the teacher and the learner, requiring us to be purposeful and intentional about prior knowledge and background knowledge. As mentioned before, the role of the teacher is in designing learning experiences that do not place the pressure of prior knowledge and background knowledge on the shoulders of the learners. Instead, the teacher meets his or her young learners where they are and then supports them as they develop their content knowledge and process skills. During the scuba diving process, rapid pressure changes can cause injuries. A diver can be injured if his or her body isn't able to adjust to the increasing (descending) pressure, the decreasing (ascending) pressure, or if these changes rapidly occur. Thus, determining learners' readiness for scuba diving is a necessary and important process.

HERE'S HOW

When the students walked into Mrs. Jones's classroom from Art class, on the whiteboard was the word *waves* and underneath this word were two columns of vocabulary words from Next Generation Science Standard 4-PS4 (NGSS Lead States, 2013).

4. Waves: Waves and Information
(4-PS4-1) Develop a model of waves to describe patterns in terms of amplitude and wavelength and that waves can cause objects to move.

Her intention is to gain insight into her students' thinking about waves and their characteristics in preparation for developing a model of waves to describe patterns in moving objects (NGSS Lead States, 2013).

WAVES	
Transverse	Longitudinal
Crest	Rarefaction
Trough	Compression
Amplitude	Amplitude
Wavelength	Wavelength
Medium	Medium

Mrs. Jones instructed the students to take out their interactive notebooks, find the next available left-side page, and spend a few minutes comparing and contrasting the two columns of words. As Mrs. Jones walked around and observed her students engaged in this process, she focused on the students' responses, or the learning outcome of prior experiences. Mrs. Jones was able to determine which students were snorkeling and which students were ready to exchange their snorkel for an oxygen tank and begin development models. Mrs. Jones values vocabulary as a necessary factor when determining prior knowledge and background knowledge. By engaging her students in this activity, she was making their thinking visible, and thus, she was able to verify what they students knew as well as determine where there were gaps and misconceptions. ∎

If you were to use a similar approach in your own classroom, would you be able to distinguish between the snorkelers and scuba divers? How do you interpret all those student responses? The answer to this question leads us to the second dimension of snorkelers and scuba divers in the classroom: the nature of their thinking.

THE NATURE OF THINKING

As Mrs. Jones observed her students' responses to the comparing and contrasting activity, she decided to elicit additional evidence about her students' thinking. With this goal in mind, she asked her students to move to the right-side of their interactive notebook. She then displayed a list of question stems and asked her students to take a moment and select two.

Question Stems	
Stop and Think Question Stems: These question stems require me to make inferences and draw conclusions. "I must STOP and think about what I know so that I can answer the question."	I wonder why… What do you think… How do you think… What would have happened if… Why do you think… Why would… How could… What if…
Search the Text and Think: These question stems require me to combine information from various sources. "I must SLOW DOWN and look in various locations to develop my answer."	Where were the differences… What was similar about… Compare… What changes… What caused…
Just Checking In: These questions just check to make sure I know the information. "I GO right to the answer."	Who… What… When… Where… Why… How…

Mrs. Jones asked the students to use the two stems they selected to design two questions of their own. After the students were given several minutes to design their questions, they exchanged their notebooks with their neighbors. Mrs. Jones provided several minutes for students to produce a written response to the questions designed by their neighbors. This activity emphasizes the observable features of student performance in Next Generation Science Standard 4-PS4 (NGSS Lead States, 2013). At the conclusion of this activity, Mrs. Jones asked her students to leave their interactive notebooks with her so that she could provide feedback to them. By purposefully and intentionally making student thinking visible with question stems and written responses, Mrs. Jones was able to reasonably and effectively identify students who were exhibiting characteristics of snorkelers or scuba divers.

Snorkelers differ from scuba divers in the qualitative nature of their thinking. Snorkelers see concepts and ideas as discrete pieces of information that they are expected to accumulate and articulate. Snorkelers do not form relationships between the concepts and ideas nor do they find the general, abstract principles that the collections of concepts or ideas represent. In some cases, snorkelers are challenged by what is and is not relevant. A snorkeler is often unable to discriminate between what is and what is not important as it relates to the science content. For example, a snorkeler may generate questions that all fall within the "Just Checking In" zone of the questions stems. Likewise, a snorkeler may list fact after fact in response to the question generated by his or her neighbor regardless of the question stem.

On the other hand, scuba divers not only see the concepts and ideas as discrete pieces of information, but they also see relationships, forming meaningful connections with the general or abstract principles under which each concept or idea fits. Scuba divers are effective and efficient in their ability to cluster concepts and ideas, organizing their thoughts and thinking based on themes and big ideas. This allows them to effectively approach each new concept with the ability to discriminate the relevant and irrelevant features and essential characteristics. Returning to the question stems, a scuba diver will most likely respond to any question by articulating relationships and big ideas.

Snorkelers prefer to view the learning from afar and treat the learning experience as an opportunity to simply see the things as objects on a checklist. After all, how can you do anything but say that you have just seen a coral reef when all you do is snorkel. Scuba divers have the pleasure of seeing the complexities of a coral reef and how it is an integral part of the aquatic ecosystem. Students with a low level of interest or students that cannot identify the relevancy of the science content often prefer to engage from afar out of fear, uncertainty, or apathy. For example, underrepresented minorities are often marginalized in science simply because their prior conceptions about science include older white men in a white lab coat. Research using the Draw a Scientist Task (DAST) shows that most individuals draw an Albert Einstein–like image when asked what they think a scientist looks like (Chambers, 1983; Finson, 2002). Why would a student commit to deep engagement (scuba diving) in a content area that they cannot see themselves pursuing beyond required coursework in K–12 schooling? Therefore, when these students are asked to scuba dive, they often resist and subsequently behaviorally, emotionally, and cognitively engage only at a surface level.

Snorkelers need access and opportunities to engage in novel, concrete, and authentic experiences that make them go, "hmm." It is this experience that helps the students understand the why behind the content, giving them a reason to explore the intricacies of the coral reef rather than the surface characteristics. Instruction should focus on encouraging individuals to scuba dive, letting them know that scuba divers never dive alone, and the boat or lead line is always there for scaffolding and support.

Do Now

Are critical thinking and risk taking encouraged in your classroom? Use the following Likert scales to examine and reflect on your ability to invite and encourage your students to move toward higher levels of thinking and learning. In your classroom, where do you fall on the following components? ■

Check List of Facts   Meaningful Connections

Got It   **Getting There**   **Not Yet**

Avoid mistakes   Mistakes as opportunities

Got It   **Getting There**   **Not Yet**

Search for correct answers   Generate and extend solutions

Got It   **Getting There**   **Not Yet**

Low levels of manipulations   Engage in physical and mental manipulations

Got It   **Getting There**   **Not Yet**

No application to authentic experiences   Clear application to authentic experiences

Got It   **Getting There**   **Not Yet**

No personal value   High personal value

Got It   **Getting There**   **Not Yet**

Learners must invest in their own learning in order to make meaning of the content. After all, you can lead students to class, but can you make them think? What strategies do you implement to create a learning experience that promotes deeper learning and thinking? As you continue to read, you will find multiple ideas and suggestions that yield increases in competence, confidence, and achievement. So, keep on divin'.

 HERE'S HOW

The students in Mr. Hutton's class were asked to select a playing card off the front table and then to sit with other students that had the same number. For example, all Jacks sit together, all 10s sit together, and so on. As they gathered around each table, Mr. Hutton gave them a blackout board.

FIGURE 1.1 Blackout Board

Questions Reading Reflections		
How did your thoughts about "Questions" change as a result of reading the article?	What information in the article challenged your beliefs?	What information within the article was a surprise or made you curious to do more research?
If you had to give this article a grade (A, B, C, D, or F), what grade would you have given the article? Why?	What questions would you like answered as a result of reading this article?	If you could provide the author of the article feedback, what specific feedback would you offer? Why?
What information within the article can be applied to your teaching career?	How did this article reinforce your existing ideas or assumptions?	How did the article mesh with your past experiences or something else you have read?

Mr. Hutton announced that the person in each group who got up the earliest this morning would begin the activity. That person was asked to select one of the nine squares and complete the thought or sentence starter. After that discussion was completed, that person would take a Post-it note and cover up the square, passing the board and the Post-it notes to the person on his or her right. The conversations would continue until either the board was complete or time expired.

Mr. Hutton strategically designed the board with relevant, thought-provoking statements that challenged the thinking of the group. At the conclusion of the group discussions, Mr. Hutton made one final request. He asked each group to summarize the complexities of their answers into one overarching, big idea. Although snorkelers prefer to see things as a discrete list of items, teachers must challenge students to see the bigger, more relevant picture. ∎

This second dimension, the nature of thinking, can induce anxiety and nervousness in both teachers and learners. For example, have you ever felt like the waves of teaching are crashing down on you? Scuba divers marvel at magnificent discoveries to be found as they explore the spectacular depths of the underwater world. Snorkelers are unable to observe the beauty from the surface and must decide to take the risk and dive in. As mentioned earlier, successfully diving in comes with safety preparation, the necessary equipment, the right location and appropriate characteristics of the diving location, and a diving buddy. Students and teachers also need to take risks, make mistakes, and explore concepts at a deeper level in order to develop a conceptual level of understanding that contains meaningful connections and multiple perspectives along with the ability to transfer that knowledge into other areas of learning. However, it is our job as teachers to ensure that when we ask students to dive in, we provide the support, or scaffolding. That is the safety preparation, the necessary equipment, the right location and appropriate diving environment, and a diving buddy. This is the nature of the interactions and the third dimension of snorkelers and scuba divers.

THE NATURE OF INTERACTIONS

You have just arrived at the Blue Heron Bridge, Riviera Beach, Florida. This location is frequently listed as one of the best diving environments in the world. However, without any prior knowledge or background knowledge and only the desire to check this off of your bucket list, you would likely have problems recognizing a flying gurnard from a bandtail sea robin. You would certainly not appreciate the unique appearance of the striated frogfish. Your interactions with your guide and diving buddy through questions, dialogue, and willingness to explore the Blue Heron Bridge would be very different if you had prior knowledge of aquatic ecosystems in this region of the world and the relationship between the various factors in this unique environment. There are many things that influence the way we interact with our environment and the people around us. Interactions are a two-way street, and it is important to pay attention to what side of the road you are on. Within any learning environment, there are many types of interactions; learner to learner, learner to instructor, learner to material, and learner to environment. Snorkelers and scuba divers interact with their peers, teachers, materials, and the environment in very different ways.

Snorkelers view interactions with peers and teachers as a means for the acquisition of key skills and knowledge. Snorkelers often view every interaction as a means to get whatever they need to get a task, assignment, or activity done. For example, a snorkeler will quickly ask, "why do we have to know about photosynthesis?" When differentiating between learned behaviors and instincts, a snorkeler will quickly ask, "is this going to be on the test?" In laboratory investigations, snorkelers strive to get the correct answer, and thus their only line of inquiry is "what do I have to do to get this right?" Teachers are viewed as "sages on the stage," and snorkelers simply want them to passively hand over the facts. Similarly, in group settings, snorkelers are often so focused on the task, that they seek only to complete each component and check it off the list.

Scuba divers take an opposite view. Scuba divers see their peers and teachers as collaborators during the learning process who provide opportunities to process, revise, and make meaning of their learning. In the classroom, scuba divers seek out opportunities for dialogue and time for engaging in ideas with other students. Referring back to the questions stems, scuba divers spend most of their time in the "Stop and Think" zone. John Hattie (2012) describes the interactions of the scuba diver through his conceptualization of an assessment-capable learner. An assessment-capable learner is aware of his or her learning and can plan the next steps with a peer or teacher. This type of learner actively engages in his or her learning by striving to make meaning of the content. Finally, this type of learner knows what the results of the assessment mean and where to go next in his or her learning. In other words, they take feedback and use it to plan the next steps in their learning. Again, scuba divers view their peers and teachers as sources of feedback so that they can further their own understanding of science skills and knowledge.

The same line of thinking can be applied to interactions between the learner and materials and the learner and the environment. Snorkelers put on their masks and snorkels and simply swim along the surface, requiring no assistance from anyone. After all, everything you expect or need to see can be seen from the surface, and there is no need to explore the depths of the water. Once you see the coral reef, you can say that you have seen the coral reef. When snorkelers get hold of an iPad or Chromebook, they see these pieces of instructional technology as simply tools for finding the right answer or surfing the web. The science-leveled readers in the reading center are simply there for a snorkeler to complete the required reading logs for the term or quarter.

The opposite is true for scuba divers. Scuba divers never dive alone, nor do they dive without the support of the team, the boat, and lead line. The team, the boat, and the lead line serve a purpose in the exploration of the environment beyond simply being required to check this item off of the bucket list. More to the point, a scuba diver's diving partner becomes a collaborator for processing and exploring the rich experiences associated with going below the surface.

Although it is accepted and expected that initially students will snorkel as they engage with new content, the opportunities teachers provide for students to interact with that content opens the door to levels of curiosity and motivation needed for deeper learning. Take a few minutes and brainstorm the multiple strategies you use to create opportunities for your student to interact with the content you are teaching. Examine each example for its ability to stimulate curiosity, trigger motivation, or leave the student wanting more. ■

 HERE'S HOW

The video Mr. Martin was about to share with his students was designed to answer the question, what material would make ice stronger? He informed his students that they needed to pay close attention to the information in the video because they were going to be asked to make and support a prediction in line with Next Generation Science Standard 5-PS1-3 (NGSS Lead States, 2013). After the video provided a brief introduction, students were presented with the following question: What material would make ice stronger: steel plates, sand, or cotton balls? Mr. Martin engaged his students in a cooperative learning activity called corners. A piece of paper with the words "steel plates" printed on it was located in one corner of the room. The piece of paper also had an image of steel plates and the Spanish translation, *acero laminado*. The word "sand," an image of sand, and *la arena* were printed on a piece of paper located in a second corner of the room. Finally, "cotton balls," an image of cotton balls, and *bolas de algodon* in a third corner. Students were instructed to move to the corner of the room that represented their prediction of what material would make ice stronger.

Each student was given the opportunity to talk with other students who had the same prediction and to share their justification. Mr. Martin not only provided an opportunity for students to share their thoughts with peers who had the same prediction, but then he opened up the conversation so each group had an opportunity to share with the other

(Continued)

groups why they believed their response was the correct prediction. Again, this strategy incorporates the observable features of student performance in Next Generation Science Standard 5-PS1 (NGSS Lead States, 2013). This strategy provided students the opportunity to interact with the teacher, the content, and their peers. The video concluded with evidence for why cotton balls was the correct response, and Mr. Martin was able to continue the lesson knowing his students wanted more. ■

Veteran divers often suggest that scuba diving is like flying underwater. They will talk and encourage other divers to go a little deeper because there are so many beautiful mysteries waiting to be discovered. Divers are often reminded that during this discovery process there are also many dangers you can't see. One of the rules of the water is never dive alone. All divers are encouraged to use the buddy system. Your buddy is truly a lifeline and a support system while under the water. So, as a teacher, how do you design and pick your diving environment? The teacher designs the interactions that will occur in the learning environment. This is done in terms of flexible groupings, who will work with whom, the structure for collaboration, how students will be held accountable for their contributions, and when you will embed the chosen strategy into your delivery.

THE JOURNEY FROM SNORKELING TO SCUBA DIVING

The students don't want to think anymore.

Nowadays students are just looking for the correct answer.

When I ask them to think critically, all I get are superficial responses.

Students don't ask good questions anymore.

Our guess is that the above observations and frustrations are not uncommon in today's classrooms and schools. Most classroom teachers have, at one time or another, experienced a similar situation and subsequent frustration, right? So, what is going on here, and what can we do about it? Put differently, the essential questions are as follows:

1. Do 21st-century learners even want to scuba dive these days?

2. Can we, as classroom teachers, move learners from snorkeling to scuba diving?

The answers to these two questions are *no* to the first question and an emphatic *yes* to the second question. Now let's unpack these responses so that by the end of this chapter we will be ready to dive into the steps necessary to take students from snorkeling to scuba diving. Let's start with; *do 21st-century learners even want to scuba dive these days?*

Up to this point in time, the research surrounding this question has been quite clear that students can and do cognitively engage in academic content at a deep level (e.g., Wang, Bergin, & Bergin, 2014; Fredericks, Blumenfeld, & Paris, 2004; Darr, 2012). Historically, the argument has been that the tsunami of technological devices and means by which we stay connected through social media and Google has limited our quest for knowledge, transforming into mere consumption of knowledge (Carr, 2010; Birkerts, 1994). Specifically, why should I commit anything to long-term memory when I can simply Google it? Thus, students have evolved into surface-level consumers of knowledge with decreasing attention spans and limited motivation to think critically, ask questions, or look for more than the correct answer. This hypothesis, too, is not supported by the most recent research on teaching, learning, and thinking (Bennett, Malton, & Kervin, 2008; Mayer, 2003).

However, what may be at play here is something completely different: not that they can't deeply engage, they just won't. If the research surrounding this first question strongly suggests that students can and do cognitively engage in academic content at a deep level, why do we not always see this in our own classrooms?

Learners selectively engage in experiences or situations that are novel, relevant, and facilitates the closing of a knowledge gap (Litman, Hutchins, & Russon, 2005; Loewenstein, 1994). Put differently, students selectively engage in eye-catching, authentic experiences, that fill in their perceived gaps in their learning. Thus, what may be happening in our classrooms is that students are not sold (i.e., no perceived learning gap, not an authentic task) on the relevancy or outcomes of the learning experiences offered in the classroom (Almarode & Miller, 2013). We have to give students a reason to scuba dive.

So, what can we do about our students' strongly held perception that what is happening in our classroom is neither relevant nor going to close a knowledge gap for them?

1. Present a clear and concise learning intention at the start of each class or lesson. This creates the perception of the knowledge gap. More on this topic in Chapter 3.

2. Provide a list of success criteria so that students are very clear about what they must know, understand, and be able to do by the end of the class or lesson. These provide a clear pathway for closing the perceived knowledge gap. Again, more on this topic in Chapter 3.

3. Make students' first exposure to the content a novel, concrete, and authentic experience that makes them go, "hmm." It is this experience that helps

students understand the why behind the content. We will dive deeper into this in Chapters 5, 6, and 7.

4. Offer multiple perspectives to the content so that students have many ways of accessing the content. These multiple perspectives are practice for applying the content to different perspectives; a precursor to deep thinking. More coming in Chapters 6 and 7.

With regard to learning intentions and success criteria, if an outsider walked into your classroom and asked a randomly selected student what he or she was learning, could the student answer the question? What if the outsider also asked the student how he or she would know he or she was successful. Could the student articulate the success criteria? Does your lesson provide opportunities for students to practice applying the content to different contexts? If you can answer each of the above questions with a definite yes, you have set the stage of deeper cognitive engagement in your classroom. Each of these ideas or strategies, when implemented into your classroom specific to your content, creates opportunities for your students to engage in novel, relevant learning experiences that close a perceived knowledge gap (Almarode & Miller, 2013).

However, we are not done yet. Setting the stage is only the first step. How do we transition to thinking critically, asking good questions, and looking for more than just the correct answer?

CAN WE MOVE LEARNERS FROM SNORKELING TO SCUBA DIVING?

To get your students to think critically and ask good questions, they have to have information about which to think critically and ask good questions. That's right, without high quality information (i.e., background knowledge and content knowledge), effective strategies for acquiring that high-quality information, and practice applying that content to other contexts, students will not be able to engage in academic content at a deep level even if you masterfully implement all four of the previously mentioned strategies: clear learning intentions, obtainable success criteria, novel experiences, and practice across different contexts.

Let's use the diving analogy to unpack the response to our second question. The act of scuba diving in a dynamic underwater environment requires the coordinated effort of people, equipment, and the environment. Scuba diving is a physically and mentally challenging task. Physically, the act of scuba diving requires the incredible delicate coordination of skills, acquired and automated only after extended periods of deliberate practice. Mentally, scuba diving requires cognitive focus and concentration aimed at blocking out distractions as well as continuous monitoring of the location and movement of other organisms in the environment to make adjustments during the dive. For the purposes of our discussion, the act of scuba diving represents the deep cognitive engagement so desperately sought after by teachers everywhere, and the environment represents the content.

For students to think critically, ask deep questions, and move beyond superficial responses, they must have content with which to work (Abrami et al., 2015; McPeck, 1981; Markman, 2012; Leslie, 2014). To return to the diving analogy, the act of scuba diving would be a waste of time and actually quite dangerous if you did not have any of the training or support for the dive (e.g., safety training, equipment, lead line, diving buddy, etc.). Similarly, asking students to think critically, ask deep questions, and move beyond superficial responses is a waste of time if these students to do not have the background knowledge or content knowledge with which to deeply engage.

Once your students do have the background knowledge or content knowledge in place, the act of deep cognitive engagement is not the next logical step. Returning to the scuba diver, to achieve even moderate levels of success, he or she must participate in deliberate practice. The students in your classroom must participate in the deliberate practice of deep cognitive engagement over an extended period of time and across multiple contexts (Abrami et al., 2015; Markman, 2012; Leslie, 2014). And, guess what? This deliberate practice can be and should be masterfully orchestrated by you through the use of intentional and purposeful strategies. As you initiate specific strategies during your classroom tasks and assignments, you are providing experiences that foster, nurture, and sustain deep cognitive engagement or not.

So, what are these intentional and purposeful strategies? To promote deep cognitive engagement of content, your questions, tasks, and assignments should do the following:

1. Align with the verb associated with the learning standard, learning intention, or success criteria. For example, if the content standard asks students to compare and contrast, does your question, task, or assignment ask them to engage at that same level, or does it ask them to simply name or identify (Almarode & Miller, 2013)? A deep dive is coming in Chapters 3, 5, and 6.

2. Require students to discuss and explain concepts to their peers. No single strategy provides a better opportunity to deeply engage in content than having to teach content to another person so that he or she understands it (Medina, 2014b). A deep dive is coming in Chapter 6.

3. Ask students to reason with evidence. Do you ask students to support their responses by explicitly asking, "what makes you say that?" A deep dive is coming in Chapters 6 and 7.

4. Offer multiple opportunities for students to make explicit connections. Using writing prompts, discussion circles, and/or graphic organizers, have students explicitly unpack how "this" relates to "that." A deep dive is coming in Chapters 6 and 7.

5. Never tell the students the whole story. Instead, provide them with opportunities to explore the data and, on their own, extract the big ideas and form conclusions. Of course, once they identify the big idea or form a conclusion, always ask "what makes you say that?" A deep dive is coming in Chapter 6.

6. Ensure that instructional experiences provide multiple exposures, through different lenses, and from different perspectives (Ritchhart, Church, & Morrison, 2011). A deep dive is coming in Chapter 7.

As you reflect on your own instructional approach, tasks, and assignments, does each instructional exercise incorporate at least one of the above six guidelines? Remember, with deep cognitive engagement, as in scuba diving, practice is required.

So here is the final thought: Not only can you lead students to class, but you also can make them think. The challenge resides in the fact that we must create engaging environments that provide relevant learning experiences, aimed at closing their perceived knowledge gaps, while at the same time orchestrating practice sessions that facilitate the development of critical thinking, good questioning, and the avoidance of superficial answers. Furthermore, this is a journey and requires patience and persistence from us, as classroom teachers, as we lead them through the progression from snorkeling to scuba diving. Making them think, transitioning them from snorkelers to scuba divers is, in the end, up to us. After all, it is all about the teacher. Now, what does the journey look like, and how do we best guide learners through the journey?

EXIT TICKET

Revisit the success criteria associated with this chapter:

1. I can compare and contrast surface-level and deep-level learners (snorkelers and scuba divers).

2. I can describe the necessary components in fostering, nurturing, and sustaining deep-level learners.

3. I can apply these components to my own classroom.

Using the following Likert scales, reflect on and evaluate your own learning. In addition to marking your level of learning on the Likert scale, provide evidence to support your self-assessment. This evidence could be a summary of your learning, examples from your own classroom, or questions that you still have about the content.

I can compare and contrast surface-level and deep-level learners (snorkelers and scuba divers).

Got It   Getting There   Not Yet

Evidence:

I can describe the necessary components in fostering, nurturing, and sustaining deep-level learners.

Got It   Getting There   Not Yet

Evidence:

I can apply these components to my own classroom.

○―――――――――――――○―――――――――――――○

Got It   **Getting There**   **Not Yet**

Evidence:

CHAPTER 2

What Does the Journey From Snorkeling to Scuba Diving Look Like?

Learning Intention

I understand the progression from snorkeling to scuba diving in science learning.

Success Criteria

By the end of this chapter, the following success criteria will be met:

1. I can compare and contrast the structure of observed learning outcomes at different points in student learning progressions.

2. I can describe the cognitive progression of learning and relate it to science learning.

3. I can relate the structure of observed learning outcomes to the balance between surface and deep learning in the classroom.

The journey from snorkeling to scuba diving is a learning journey. As mentioned in the previous chapter, this is a journey that requires patience and persistence on our part, as classroom teachers, as we guide learners through the progression from snorkeling to scuba diving. Richard Mayer (2011) defines learning as "change in knowledge attributable to experience (p. 14)." Mayer (2011) goes on to unpack this definition through the eyes of the learner, not singularly from the perspective of the teacher. That is, learning is a change in what the learner understands, knows, and is able to do as a result of some experience. Consider a fourth-grade student whose success criteria derived from the Next Generation Science Standard 4-PS4-1 is to develop a model of waves to describe patterns in terms of amplitude and wavelength (NGSS Lead States, 2013).

4. Waves: Waves and Information
(4-PS4-1) Develop a model of waves to describe patterns in terms of amplitude and wavelength and that waves can cause objects to move

Our goal, as the classroom teacher, is to create an educational experience that fosters, nurtures, and sustains a change in what the learner knows about the components and characteristics of waves. Furthermore, the experience should promote an understanding of the cause-and-effect relationships between amplitude, wavelength, and the movement of the medium and objects. Finally, the experience should prepare the learner to use models to explain cause-and-effect relationships and the description of a system through components and interactions (NGSS Lead States, 2013): know, understand, and be able to do.

What is missing from the above example is a focus on the learner regarding the three dimensions from Chapter 1 that are associated with snorkelers and scuba divers: prior and background knowledge, the nature of students' thinking, and the nature of the interactions. So how does a learner progress from snorkeling to scuba diving, and what role does prior and background knowledge, the nature of students' thinking, and the nature of the interactions play in this progression? As a classroom teacher, we might phrase it this way: "Where do I start?"

If attention is solely focused on what the teacher does, then we fall into the trap of placing all of the pressure on the learner (i.e., placing the pressure of prior knowledge and background knowledge on the shoulders of the divers instead of meeting them where they are and supporting them as the dive). For example, can you think of a learner that would find it difficult to name or list parts of a wave? How about a learner that would find it difficult to articulate how changes in the amplitude or wavelength change the wave? Thus, without success in the two previously mentioned tasks, constructing a model and using the model in explanations would be well above the appropriate level of challenge for a learner.

Do Now

Consider 4-PS4-1. What prior or background knowledge would a learner need to have in order to successfully meet the standard? What type of thinking is required to successfully meet the standard? Describe the potential interactions that would occur in this standard? How would you know where to start in creating the experience described by Mayer (2011)?

So how does a learner progress from snorkeling to scuba diving, and what role does prior and background knowledge, the nature of students' thinking, and the nature of the interactions play in this progression? As a classroom teacher, we might phrase it this way: "Where do I start?" Keeping in mind that the definition of learning is from the perspective of the learner and not the teacher, we must avoid first looking at what we are doing as teachers and, instead, look at what the students are doing. That is, the focus should be on the observable thinking of the students in the classroom. If you want to know about a learner's prior and background knowledge, the nature of students' thinking, and how the nature of the interactions play in this progression, look at what they are producing as they make their thinking visible.

 HERE'S HOW

Miss Didlake has designed an exit slip asking her fourth graders to summarize their learning on pitch and frequency, NGSS 4-PS4-1.

3. Waves: Waves and Information
(4-PS4-1) Develop a model of waves to describe patterns in terms of amplitude and wavelength and that waves can cause objects to move

Specifically, Miss Didlake is trying to understand her students' thinking about using models of waves to describe patterns in terms of amplitude and wavelength (NGSS Lead States, 2013). She asks her students to illustrate the connection between the parts of a wave and the pitch and volume of a sound wave.

STUDENT WORK SAMPLES

FIGURE 2.1   Student Work Sample #1

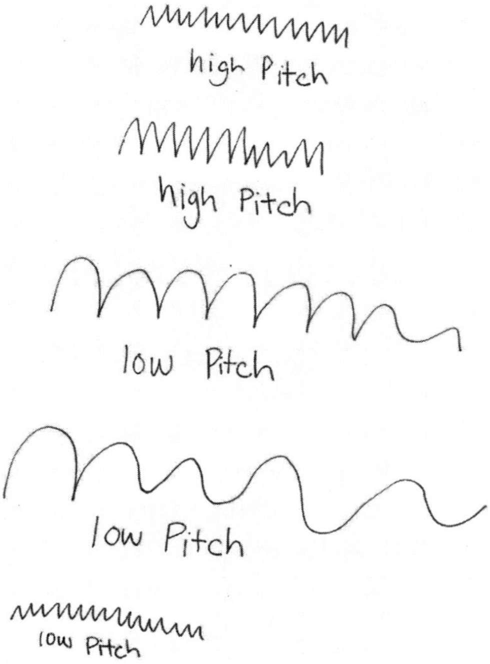

high Pitch

high Pitch

low Pitch

low Pitch

low Pitch

FIGURE 2.2   Student Work Sample #2

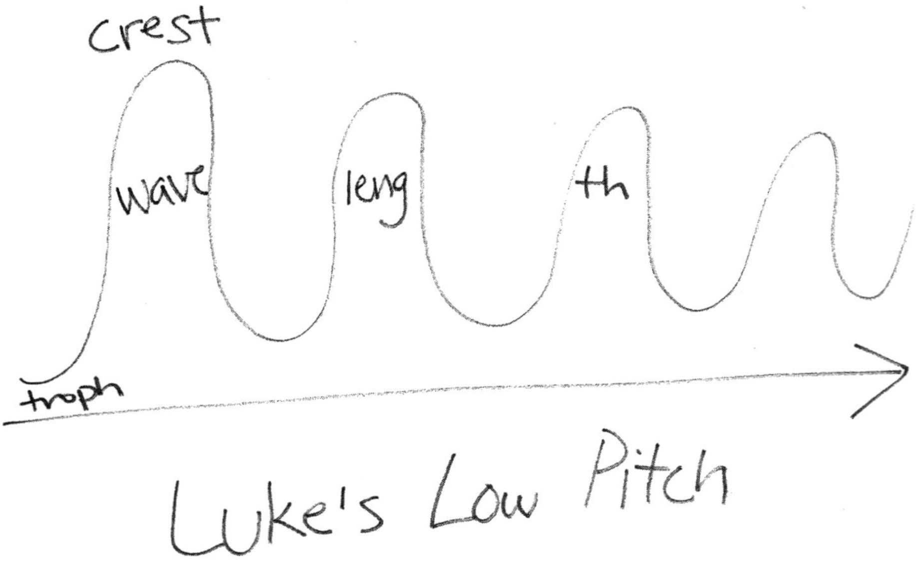

crest

wave leng th

troph

Luke's Low Pitch

FIGURE 2.3   Student Work Sample #3

loud High frequency

quiet high pitched frequency

loud low frequency

quiet low pitched frequency

Do Now

Looking at these three student responses to the exit ticket, and analyze the three work samples based on the following items:

1. Prior and background knowledge of the students: What do the students' responses suggest about their prior and background knowledge?

2. Nature of the thinking: What are the differences in the three student responses?

3. Nature of the interactions: What are the differences in the ways in which each student interacted with the exit ticket?

Using these three questions to unpack the three dimensions of snorkelers and scuba divers provides insight into the current level of thinking for each of your students by making their prior or background knowledge, current level of understanding, and the interaction between the student and the exit ticket visible. However, what to do with this information is infinitely more important if we are to then make purposeful and intentional decisions about where to go next in their learning journey or progression. So, how do we make sense of student thinking?

In the late 1970s and early 1980s, researchers engaged in a similar exercise as above, only they looked at many more work samples and across several disciplines such as mathematics, English, and geography (Biggs & Collis, 1982; Kirby & Biggs, 1981). Focusing primarily on student work, researchers noted five distinct patterns in the variation of student thinking. For example, some of the learners' responses were incoherent or missed the point of the assignment. In their responses, these learners focused on irrelevant facts, concepts, or ideas. From the exit slips in Miss Didlake's class, did any of the three students focus on irrelevant information?

Biggs and Collis (1982) also found that other students focused on a single idea or one relevant aspect of the content, omitting other details in their responses. A third group of learners included several relevant but independent aspects of the content. That is, these leaners provided lists or serial lists of information without linking the concepts, whereas some of the students were able to identify relationships between the facts, concepts, or ideas, moving beyond simply listing discrete pieces of information. The final group of students produced responses that generalized the content to a new domain, extending their learning to abstract principles or generalizable ideas. Again, from the exit slips in Miss Didlake's class, which group did her three learners most resemble?

THE STRUCTURE OF OBSERVED LEARNING OUTCOMES (SOLO TAXONOMY)

From these five distinct patterns in the structure of thinking, Biggs and Collis (1982) developed a model known as the Structure of Observed Learning Outcomes, or SOLO Taxonomy. This model is based on levels of thinking that can be observed and become increasingly more complex and difficult. In other words, the SOLO Taxonomy helps us make sense of learners' prior and background knowledge, the nature of students' thinking, and the nature of the interactions.

The SOLO Taxonomy is almost universally identified and represented by the below visual representation.

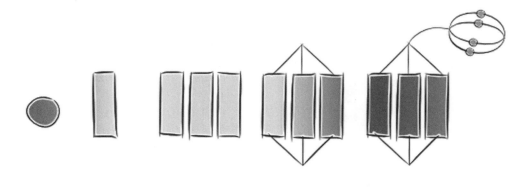

SOURCE: SOLO Symbol Images © Hook Education Ltd. Reproduced with permission.

THE PROGRESSION THROUGH THE SOLO TAXONOMY

Using this visual representation, let's briefly walk through the progression of thinking in the SOLO Taxonomy from left to right, using examples from different areas of the Next Generation Science Standards. For a particular science concept or idea, learners may have no prior knowledge or experience with the information and thus have no relevant structure to their thinking (the dot). This is referred to as the prestructural level or prestructural thinking. Learners may focus on irrelevant ideas or avoid engaging in the content, requiring the teacher to support the learner in acquiring and building background knowledge. This type of thinking manifests itself several ways in the classroom.

While at morning meeting, Ms. Hyson asks her kindergartners to make observations about the following photograph (NGSS K-ESS2-2) (NGSS Lead States, 2013).

FIGURE 2.5

A prestructural learner may respond with a story that is only tangentially related to the question. That is, the young learner may tell a tale of his "Meemaw" and that she has trees at her house. Although important to the learner, the information revealed by this student making his thinking visible is more important to the teacher. He or she now has information that informs his or her next steps in instruction: scaffolding the learner to identify the relevant details of the photograph. A second response might be silence or disengagement. However, with the SOLO Taxonomy in mind, the interpretation of the students' responses by the teacher is not limited to "the students just don't or won't behave or participate." Instead, the learners are likely at the prestructural level, not sure what Ms. Hyson means by "make observations," and the learning experience should aim to move them to unistructural and multistructural thinking.

As the learners progress in their thinking, they may have a single idea or component related to the concept, represented by the single rectangle. This is referred to as the unistructural level of thinking. Learners at this level identify, name, and follow simple procedures (Hook & Mills, 2011). Referring back to the photograph, a student may identify "a plant," "it is green," or "that is a road or sidewalk." In multistructural thinking, learners then begin to acquire multiple ideas (three rectangles) that are combined into a coherent description. For example, "that is a plant pushing through a sidewalk."

When learners are identifying relationships between concepts or ideas (three connected rectangles), they are said to be at the relational level or engaged in relational thinking. In Ms. Hyson's classroom, this learner might state "the plant, as it began to grow, broke through the pavement." In this case, the learner has related the growth or change in the plant to the break or change in the sidewalk. The next step in the SOLO progression is for the learner to transfer learning to different contexts (three connected rectangles with the extension). At the extended abstract level of thinking, learners formulate big ideas and generalize their learning to a new domain (Hook & Mills, 2011, 2012; Martin, 2012). For example, an extended abstract thinker in Ms. Hyson's classroom might ask about the consequences of roads and sidewalks being built near forests. Learners at this level may begin to generalize this to a human having to wear larger clothing sizes as he or she grows from a baby to a kindergartner or storing food in a refrigerator. The big idea, of course, is animals and plants change the environment to meet their needs (NGSS Lead States, 2013).

Do Now

Using the visual representation from Figure 2.4 (see p. 35) and knowing that *the SOLO taxonomy is the framework for the journey from snorkeling to scuba diving*, where do you draw the line? Where in the progression do learners make the transition from snorkeling to scuba diving?

Do Now

Think-Produce-Explain.

Think: Take several minutes to think through the progression of thinking in the SOLO Taxonomy. Put the book down, and think through the information in the previous section (e.g., take a walk, get a coffee, let the dog out).

(Continued)

(Continued)

Produce: Using the below visual representation of the SOLO Taxonomy, produce evidence of your thinking: label, summarize, outline, and so on.

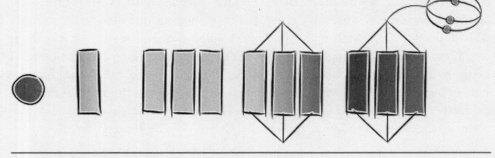

SOURCE: SOLO Symbol Images © Hook Education Ltd. Reproduced with permission.

Explain: Find a mentor, colleague, or friend, and explain the SOLO Taxonomy to him or her. Try to limit your explanation to a few minutes.

Speaking of examples, lets revisit Ms. Didlake's exit ticket on waves.

HERE'S HOW

What would each level of the SOLO look like with regard to student responses to the exit ticket? Ms. Didlake mapped out student responses she expected at each level of the SOLO Taxonomy. Did your responses to the above three prompts change in light of your new learning?

Prestructural thinking	The student did not respond or provided irrelevant information.
Unistructural thinking	The student identifies one part of a wave or one characteristic of a wave (e.g., crest or trough, amplitude, or wavelength).
Multistructural thinking	The student identifies most or all of the parts of a wave and all characteristics of a wave.
Relational thinking	The student relates amplitude to volume and pitch to frequency, OR the student relates amplitude to crest and frequency to wavelength.
Extended abstract thinking	The student connects pitch and frequency to the hearing range of different species of animals and the physiology of their ears.

Do Now

Now, how would you classify these three additional student work samples? Justify your response with specifics from each student's work sample.

MORE STUDENT WORK SAMPLES

FIGURE 2.6   Student Work Sample #1

FIGURE 2.7   Student Work Sample #2

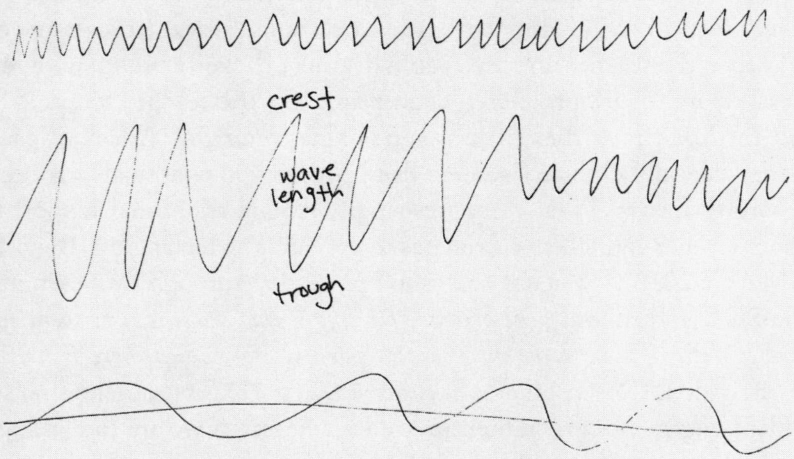

(Continued)

(Continued)

FIGURE 2.8   Student Work Sample #3

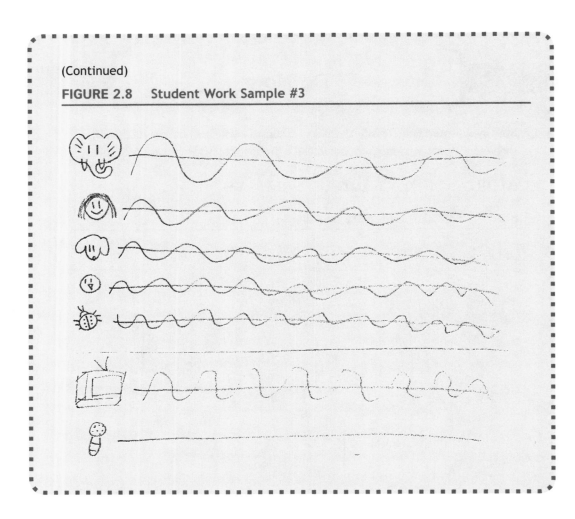

As a word of caution, the representation of the SOLO Taxonomy is linear. However, the progression is cyclic. For example, learners may be engaged in a learning experience focusing on identifying relationships among ideas (three connected rectangles), when the teacher notices a gap in learners' background knowledge. Thus, it is necessary, and developmentally appropriate, for the teacher to circle back and support the learners as they fill this gap (single rectangle). A lack of background knowledge does not exclude a student from engaging in relational learning. Neither does a wrong answer. These responses simply require additional support from the classroom teacher and fellow classmates to provide "the rectangles" (Biggs & Collis, 1982; Martin, 2012). "When it comes to progressing through this learning journey and the SOLO Taxonomy, *the primary finding is this, student time spent engaged in relevant content appears to be an essential variable for which there is no substitute*" [emphasis added] (Rosenshine & Berliner, 1978, p. 12). Thus, there is no substitute for student engagement in authentic science learning if we are to develop higher-order thinking and transfer of knowledge to other contexts in our classrooms.

Select an assignment, activity, or task that you have used or will use in your science instruction. Of course, this assignment, activity, or task must provide opportunities for students to make their thinking visible and thus should involve open-ended questions or prompts. Then, select one of the following options:

Option #1: Using the blank table below, describe the student responses you would expect at each level of the SOLO Taxonomy. This is for upcoming assignments, activities, or tasks.

Option #2: Analyze student responses and organize them based on the level of thinking. Summarize the responses at each level of the SOLO Taxonomy. This is for already accomplished assignments, activities, or tasks.

	OBSERVED LEVEL OF THINKING
Prestructural thinking	
Unistructural thinking	
Multistructural thinking	
Relational thinking	
Extended abstract thinking	

WHY THE SOLO TAXONOMY?

There are five important features of the SOLO Taxonomy that make it particularly unique and powerful for classroom teachers as they foster, nurture, and sustain learners *to obtain higher-order thinking, high levels of engagement, and the transfer of knowledge to other contexts.* First, the SOLO Taxonomy is the only framework or taxonomy for learning and thinking that is supported by cognitive science and the science of how we learn (Biggs & Collis, 1982; Hook & Mills, 2011, 2012; Kirby & Biggs, 1981; Martin, 2012). Yes, the only one. We will address this further in the next chapter. Second, the model requires that students engage in multiple opportunities to make their thinking visible. A classroom that does not provide multiple opportunities for students to make their thinking visible provides little insight into where students are in their learning journey. For example, classrooms that are 70 percent to

80 percent teacher talk leave little time for teachers to capture student thinking. Thus, the journey from snorkeler to scuba diver is both unclear and likely left to chance. Third, the ability for students to identify relationships among facts, concepts, or ideas and the ability for students to extend their thinking requires that they know the ideas that they are expected to relate and extend (e.g., prior knowledge and background knowledge). Asking students to identify the relationship between pitch and frequency or amplitude and volume when they do not have independently secure knowledge and understanding of those ideas is diving too fast and comes with significant risk.

Fourth, learners can and do begin at different levels of the SOLO Taxonomy for different content areas and across different topics within a content. There is no one universal starting point, and that starting point is not based on a label. A learner may be an extended abstract thinker in mathematics but engage in multistructural thinking in science. A learner could engage in prestructural thinking in reading and extended abstract thinking in science. Likewise, within science, a learner could engage in prestructural thinking with regard to organisms and ecosystems but extended abstract thinking in space systems.

For example, a learner who has significant prior experiences, and thus prior and background knowledge with constellations, stars, and the solar system, may immediately be able to extend his or her thinking when introduced to the Next Generation Science Standard 5-ESS1-1, to support an argument that the apparent brightness of the sun and stars is due to their relative distances from the Earth.

5. Space Systems: Stars and the Solar System
(5-ESS1-1) Support an argument that differences in the apparent brightness of the sun compared to other stars and due to their relative distances from the Earth.

However, when learning to develop a model to describe the movement of matter among plants, animals, decomposers, and the environment, 5-LS2-1, he or she may have no prior or background knowledge and thus begin with identifying or describing individual aspects of the model.

5. Matter and Energy in Organisms and Ecosystems
(5-LS2-1) Support an argument that plants get the materials they need for growth chiefly from air and water.

Finally, the SOLO Taxonomy is inclusive. Rather than focusing on labels, individual, and background characteristics, the SOLO Taxonomy focuses on thinking. Learners at all ages can progress from snorkeling to scuba diving. Kindergarteners can engage in extended abstract thinking just as quickly as an adult can engage in prestructural thinking. The implication of this aspect of the SOLO Taxonomy is that all learners can be scuba divers. All means all!

SCUBA DIVING FOR ALL LEARNERS

Learners in our science classrooms are from all different walks of life and are at different locations in their journey from snorkeling to scuba diving. As teachers, we strive to create and provide educational experiences where (1) all learners are active participants in their science learning and (2) all learners are given support and offered opportunities to be successful. These are the mindsets for meaningful, intentional, inclusive practices in the science classroom. So, *how do we successfully provide an inclusive science learning environment that actively engages learners from all different walks of life taking into consideration where they are in their learning journey from snorkeling to scuba diving?*

Successful inclusive practices are wholly dependent on the supports teachers can provide learners. Without a meaningful and intentional scaffold in place intended to move each learner from facts (surface knowledge) to generalized and abstract knowledge (understanding or deep knowledge) educators run the risk of missing those learning opportunities that further a learner's understanding, facilitate meaningful connections with prior knowledge, and promote higher-order thinking. This is the kind of deep understanding that we, as educators, want for each of our learners regardless of their racial or ethnic background, socioeconomic status, or ability status. If you take it one step further and combine those learning experiences with feedback, this will allow students to grow, manipulate, and extend knowledge that they then own and use in innumerable situations and contexts.

However, this is easier said than done and leaves many teachers unsure about how to meet this challenge amidst the other demands of being a classroom teacher in the 21st century. For example, some classroom teachers focus on student labels (i.e., poor, learning disabled, autistic, below grade level, etc.), unintentionally isolating learners from this access to information, experiences, and opportunities in the classroom based on preconceived notions about what the learner can and cannot do. This is detrimental to student learning, specifically students' progression from snorkeling to scuba diving.

> The solution is to shift our focus from categorizing, classifying, or labeling learners based on demographic, background, and disability characteristics, and, instead, focus on the structure of their observed learning outcomes: the nature of their thinking. We make this shift using the SOLO Taxonomy. (Biggs & Collis, 1982)

The SOLO Taxonomy provides teachers with a framework for classifying student thinking in terms of quantity and quality, not in terms of overgeneralized characteristics associated with a student's eligibility criteria (e.g., what they can or can't do because of, say, a diagnosed learning disability).

Revisit the question stems on p. 15 in the previous chapter. How does the SOLO Taxonomy provide a framework for understanding student thinking in terms of quantity and quality for the interactive notebook activity in Mrs. Jones's classroom?

Determining the correct level of difficulty is often determined through the process of assessing students' prior or background knowledge. The goal, of course, is to use this information to establish a level of challenge that will stimulate effort. Developmentally appropriate, in this case, means teaching one step beyond the learner's current level of thinking, also known as the "plus one rule" (Biggs & Collis, 1982). The real reward comes when the student is successful in putting forth the effort to meet the challenge. If the activity or task is overwhelmingly difficult, learners most likely will not put forth the effort to complete the task.

HERE'S HOW

If a third-grade teacher asks her students to complete a cause-and-effect thinking map for a particular habitat, students would need to explore relationships within that particular habitat (relational) and, likely, hypothesize about the certain effects or outcomes (extended abstract).

FIGURE 2.9

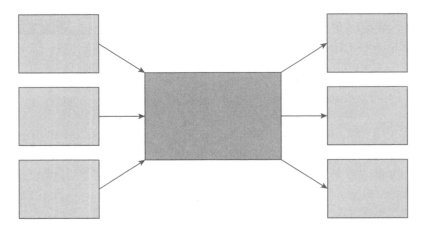

This would be overwhelming for a learner at the unistructural level who is *not yet* able to name or list characteristics of organisms or components of a habitat. Similarly, a learner who is ready to engage in relational thinking (e.g., explain causes and justify) but is only expected to name or list characteristics of organisms or components of a habitat will also likely not put forth the effort to complete the task. In this second example, the activity or task is below the learner's level of thinking.

Using the well-known book, *The Lorax*, by Dr. Seuss, look at the following example of a cause-and-effect map that scaffolds thinking to the "plus one rule."

FIGURE 2.10

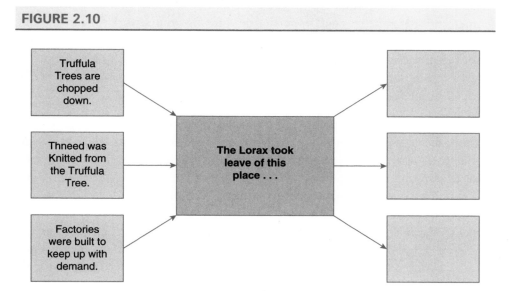

Ultimately, we want to offer students appropriate levels of productive tension, enough to stimulate curiosity and determination yet keeping the learning intention within reach so the students put forth effort. After all, true motivation results when effort is made to accomplish a challenging task and there is a successful result. Most teachers regulate the productive tension through interactions like proximity, visibility, time, and conditions tied to the activities or tasks they offer their students. Academically, we are continually scaffolding our content by adjusting the cognitive demand within the students' learning experiences. The SOLO Taxonomy is capable of being the decision-making tool that can assist teachers when determining that one step beyond their students' current level of difficulty. Therefore, "developmentally appropriate" means teaching one step beyond the learners' current level of thinking, also known as the "plus one rule" (Biggs & Collis, 1982).

Assessing prior knowledge and level of thinking depends on the students' responses to classroom strategies or activities. The goal, again, is to use this understanding of student thinking to design educational experiences that give them access to developmentally appropriate information, experiences, and opportunities coupled with effective feedback and extension that allow for them to grow knowledge that they then own, manipulate, and use in innumerable situations and contexts, and to which they can add more information, experiences, and opportunities.

The SOLO Taxonomy provides this scaffolding for teachers in a meaningful way. The possibilities of teaching and learning based on the nature of learners' thinking rather than on "ability" provide teachers flexibility to facilitate the development of new knowledge amongst learners. Learners experience natural ways to extend their understanding through intentional opportunities to connect new information with prior understanding regardless of how simple or complex. This can mean entrée, and thus inclusion, into science learning for all learners. Shifting the lens from what a learner can or cannot do to the place on the SOLO Taxonomy where that learner's prior experiences and opportunities provide groundwork for moving into increasingly complex understanding demands that educators see strengths and potential in each learner. This approach allows for each learner to also serve as a teacher to others as they are all acquiring and attaching new information to existing knowledge (i.e., the diving buddy).

Most importantly, the taxonomy prepares teachers for collecting meaningful information about student thinking that informs their next steps. Formative and authentic assessments that make student thinking visible allows teachers to ask the most important, and often absent, "so what?" question about what learners know and are able to do. For instance, when a learner demonstrates a relational understanding of density and volume, we cannot assume that means the student possesses a relational understanding of standard and nonstandard units of measure. Therefore, assessing a learner's prior knowledge and level of thinking for each new chunk of content (objectives) drives the learning progression. With meaningful evidence of student thinking in hand, teachers are armed to guide their learners from snorkelers to scuba divers.

Learners come into learning opportunities with an assumption of strength as the teacher assesses for prior knowledge and nature of their thinking rather than assuming this level of readiness based on prior experiences with the learners or on the learners' labels. This strengths-based approach to learner outcomes envelops learners of differing abilities because differences in prior knowledge and nature of thinking are assumed within the model.

Have you ever wanted to learn how to scuba dive? The process for learning to scuba dive provides a concrete example of how the SOLO Taxonomy can guide teaching and learning in science. Did you know that when people first learn to dive often times they begin in a swimming pool? Imagine standing chest deep in warm, turquoise waters with a scuba diving regulator in hand while being told to put your face in the water. This can be counterintuitive to the first-time diver. To be honest, many learners have no idea what to expect as they learn to scuba dive or learn about how forces interact with objects to change their speed and direction as in Next Generation Science Standard K-PS2-2.

K. Forces and Interactions: Pushes and Pulls
(K-PS2-2) Analyze data to determine if a design solution works as intended to change the speed or direction of an object with a push or a pull.

For this reason, scuba courses, and science, are best taught in steps or chunks. Your students may not yet be ready to jump off the boat into a particular topic. Determining where your students are in the learning progression and where they go next could very well determine your instructional effectiveness as well as their academic success. This leads us to the first component of the instructional framework for moving students from snorkelers to scuba divers: young learners must acquire high quality information. Emphasizing a standards-based approach, readers will experience the process of identifying the priority standards in elementary science and how to unpack those standards, readying them for the learning journey and progression from snorkeling to scuba diving.

EXIT TICKET

Revisit the success criteria associated with this chapter:

1. I can compare and contrast the structure of observed learning outcomes at different points in student learning progressions.

2. I can describe the cognitive progression of learning and relate it to science learning.

3. I can relate the structure of observed learning outcomes to the balance between surface and deep learning in the classroom.

Using the following Likert scales, reflect on and evaluate your own learning:

I can compare and contrast the structure of observed learning outcomes at different points in student learning progressions.

○————————————————○————————————————○

Got It   **Getting There**   **Not Yet**

Evidence:

I can describe the cognitive progression of learning and relate it to science learning.

Got It   Getting There   Not Yet

Evidence:

I can relate the structure of observed learning outcomes to the balance between surface and deep learning in the classroom.

Got It   Getting There   Not Yet

Evidence:

Revisit the Do-Now from early in the chapter. Where do you now draw the line? Where in the progression do learners make the transition from snorkeling to scuba diving? Then, using the SOLO Taxonomy and your own experiences and examples, compare and contrast snorkelers and scuba divers using the following Venn Diagram.

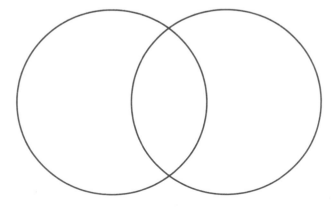

CHAPTER 3

From Snorkelers to Scuba Divers

Step #1—Acquiring High Quality Information

Learning Intention

I understand that science standards identify high quality information that learners must know and understand as they move through the science learning progression.

Success Criteria

By the end of this chapter, the following success criteria will be met:

1. I can explain how to unpack a science standard.

2. I can describe the balance between surface and deep learning within a science standard.

3. I can explain the relationship between unpacking a science standard, the acquisition of high quality information, and science learning progressions.

Let's review. Up to this point, there are three main ideas that you should keep in your working memory, or oxygen tank:

1. In our classroom, there are snorkelers, and there are scuba divers.

2. The SOLO Taxonomy is the framework for the journey from snorkeler to scuba diver.

3. We, as classroom teachers, can provide learning experiences that foster, nurture, and sustain deep cognitive engagement that results in scuba divers.

Do Now

Take a few moments and return back to the previous chapters containing these main ideas. Justify why each of these three statements is considered a main idea. If during the deep dive into the previous chapters you extracted a different set of main ideas, argue your point as well. ■

THE INSTRUCTIONAL FRAMEWORK

Determining where your students are in the learning progression, how they are making meaning of their learning, and thus where they will or should go next in their learning could very well determine your instructional effectiveness as well as their academic success. As promised in the introduction of this book, we will present an instructional framework that fosters, nurtures, and sustains the level of engagement necessary for learners to successfully navigate any learning progression in science. This instructional framework has three components (adapted from Markman, 2012):

1. Young learners must acquire high quality information.

2. Young learners must experience evidence-based strategies in the science learning environment.

3. Young learners must have practice applying that content to other contexts.

The first component of the instructional framework for moving students from snorkelers to scuba divers, young learners must acquire high quality information, requires us, the classroom teachers, to have a clear understanding of the learning progression for each and every science topic. Teachers must know exactly what students must know, understand, and be able to do within each standard. In addition, teachers must develop learning progressions for learners so that regardless of their starting points, the journey from snorkeling to scuba diving is clear.

This is accomplished by unpacking the standards. Emphasizing a standards-based approach, unpacking the standards is an efficient and effective process for readying the content for the learning journey and progression from snorkeling to scuba diving (Ainsworth, 2003, 2010). Unpacking the standards provides a clear path forward in the journey from snorkeling to scuba diving. Once this pathway is clear to the teacher, big ideas, essential questions, learning intentions, success criteria, and engaging scenarios (hook) provide authenticity that initially engages the learner and subsequently nurtures and sustains that engagement. In other words, it motivates the potential scuba diver by giving a reason or relevant excuse/purpose to leave the beach, shoreline, or boat and jump into the water. After all, if the potential scuba diver will not even get into the water, this will be a short journey with no progress.

However, let's be clear about two misconceptions associated with unpacking the standards:

1. Unpacking the standards is NOT simply identifying items from the standards.

2. Unpacking the standards involves focusing in on the level of thinking expected in the standard so that the learning experiences align with this level of thinking or supporting students as they move toward this level of thinking.

Do Now

In the space provided jot down a response to the following questions;

- Teachers often make decisions about what their students really need to know. So, what is the difference between **need** to know and **neat** to know?

- What do you believe students **need** to know, understand, and be able to do in your science classroom?

- How is this different from what is **neat** to know, understand, and be able to do?

- How do you make decisions about what to teach? ∎

Unpacking the standards provides a clear path forward by allowing classroom teachers to see what students *need* to know, understand, and be able to do while at the same time providing teachers the opportunity to make conscious decisions to stay the course and to avoid the distractions and digressions of what is just *neat* to know, understand, and be able to do.

The Big Idea
*Unpacking the standards allows us to differentiate what students **need** to know from what is simply **neat** to know.*

NEED VERSUS NEAT TO KNOW

The Next Generation Science Standards (NGSS) were constructed with this in mind and use the *coning effect* (NGSS Lead States, 2013; National Research Council, 2012). The coning effect is a vertical progression of standards from simple to complex and concrete to abstract. Within each Next Generation Science Standard is a clear presentation of what learners *need* to know, understand, and be able to do to meet that particular standard.

 HERE'S HOW

Below you will find the kindergarten standard for Weather and Climate.

K. Weather and Climate
(K-PS3-1) Make observations to determine the effect of sunlight on Earth's surface.*
(K-PS3-2) Use tools and materials to design and build a structure that will reduce the warming effect of sunlight on an area.
(K-ESS2-1) Use and share observations of local weather conditions to describe patterns over time.

This information, along with the Science and Engineering Practices, Disciplinary Core Ideas, and Crosscutting Concepts, spell out expectations of what students should know, understand, and be able to do. ∎

---

*You can view the entire Next Generation Science Standards for K. Weather and Climate at https://www.nextgenscience.org/topic-arrangement/kweather-and-climate

Again, this is a presentation of what learners *need* to know, understand, and be able to do to meet this particular standard.

Based on the above K. Weather and Climate standard, label each topic or idea either <u>needs</u> to know or <u>neat</u> to know based on what the standards says a kindergartner **needs** to know about weather and climate. ∎

TOPIC OR IDEA	NEED OR NEAT
Reading a thermometer	
Climate change	
Weather data	
Effects of sunlight	
Local weather forecast	
Season differences in hemispheres	

Reading a thermometer, weather data, effects of sunlight, and local weather forecast are all **need** to know while the remaining topics are simply **neat** to know. Although the **neat** to know topics are no less important, they are better explored in subsequent lessons. Where exactly depends on the *Articulation of Disciplinary Core Ideas (DCIs) across grade levels*. Let's sort that out next.

VERTICAL AND HORIZONTAL PROGRESSIONS

The standards also provide connections between the particular standard and other science standards in that grade level as well as the vertical progression of standards from simple to complex and concrete to abstract in later grade levels. In the example below, *Connections to other DCIs in kindergarten* represents connections between the particular standard and other science standards in that grade level while the *Articulation of DCIs across grade levels* represents the vertical progression of standards from simple to complex and concrete to abstract. The *Connections to other DCIs in kindergarten* as well as the particular standard provides the information needed to develop the progression from snorkeler to scuba diver. The *Articulation of DCIs across grade levels*, or vertical progression, provides the starting and stopping points in that grade level.

Connections to other DCIs in kindergarten: K.ETS1.A (K-PS3-2), (K-ESS3-2)
Articulation of DCIs across grade-levels: 1.PS4.B (K-PS3-1), (K-PS3-2); 2.ESS1.C (K-ESS3-2)

Do Now

Complete the following table with your own thinking about standards. Visit http://www.nextgenscience.org to find specific examples for the third column of the table. ■

CONCEPT OR IDEA	SUMMARY	EXAMPLE FROM THE NGSS
The coning effect		
Vertical progression		
Horizontal progression		
Need versus neat		
No personal value		

As committed professionals, we often feel as if there are other things that students should learn about weather in kindergarten. In a standards-based approach, this is just *neat* to know, understand, and be able to do and should be cleared from the progression. With the coning effect, we trust that our colleagues in subsequent grades will take care of vertical progression while we focus on the horizontal progression in our own classroom. Together, the Next Generation Science Standards offer the tools for providing a clear path forward in the journey from snorkeling to scuba diving. Next up is the unpacking of the standard.

UNPACKING THE STANDARD

First, let's go through all of the steps within the process. This process will work regardless of whether your state, district, or school uses the Next Generation Science Standards or state-level and district-level standards (e.g., Virginia uses their own standards of learning and not the NGSS). After we move through each step, we will examine two examples and create essential questions for your classroom that motivate the potential scuba diver by giving a reason or relevant excuse/purpose to leave the beach, shoreline, or boat and jump into the water.

Steps to unpacking (for additional resources see Ainsworth 2003; 2010):

1. Select a specific NGSS standard for a specific science content that you are preparing to teach.

3. Forces and Interactions
(3-PS2-1) Plan and conduct an investigation to provide evidence of the effects of balanced and unbalanced forces on the motion of an object.
(3-PS2-2) Make observations and/or measurements of an object's motion to provide evidence that a pattern can be used to predict future motion.

2. Within a standard there are important nouns that represent the ideas, concepts, or topics students must learn. Nouns are vocabulary, ideas, concepts, and topics within the standard. Underline the nouns within the standard.

3. Forces and Interactions
(3-PS2-1) Plan and conduct an <u>investigation</u> to provide <u>evidence</u> of the <u>effects</u> of <u>balanced</u> and <u>unbalanced forces</u> on the <u>motion</u> of an <u>object</u>.

3. Take the underlined nouns and arrange them in a way that you believe represents a logical progression for learning these ideas, concepts, or topics. This, of course relies on your professional judgment and how you believe it is best to approach this particular standard.

PROGRESSION OF IDEAS, CONCEPTS, OR TOPICS (NOUNS)
Object's motion
Observations and measurements
Balanced and unbalanced forces
Effects of balanced and unbalanced forces
Observations and measurements as evidence
Future motion
Electric and magnetic interactions (magnets)
Cause and effect relationships
Objects in contact versus not in contact with each other
Simple design problem

Again, this represents the learning progression of ideas, concepts, or topics for NGSS 3-PS2. However, up to this point in the unpacking process, we do not know the depth at which learners must engage with these ideas, concepts, or topics.

4. Verbs represent the depth at which learners must engage with these ideas, concepts, or topics. Circle the relevant verbs within the standard.

3. Forces and Interactions
(3-PS2-1) Plan and conduct an <u>investigation</u> to provide <u>evidence</u> of the <u>effects</u> of <u>balanced</u> and <u>unbalanced forces</u> on the <u>motion</u> of an <u>object</u>.

5. Take the circled verbs and match them with their associated or linked ideas, concepts, or topics. The pathway to scuba diving is almost complete.

PROGRESSION OF IDEAS, CONCEPTS, OR TOPICS (NOUNS)	DEPTH OF ENGAGEMENT (VERBS)
Object's motion	Make
Observations and measurements	Make
Balanced and unbalanced forces	Provide
Effects of balanced and unbalanced forces	Provide
Observations and measurements as evidence	Make
Future motion	Predict
Electric and magnetic interactions (magnets)	Determine
Cause and effect relationships	Ask Determine
Objects in contact versus not in contact with each other	Ask Determine
Simple design problem	Define Solve Apply

6. Finally, using both the standard and the SOLO Taxonomy, match the verb with the level of thinking expected in the standard.

PROGRESSION OF IDEAS, CONCEPTS, OR TOPICS (NOUNS)	DEPTH OF ENGAGEMENT (VERBS)
Object's motion	Make (multistructural)
Observations and measurements	Make (multistructural)
Balanced and unbalanced forces	Provide (multistructural)
Effects of balanced and unbalanced forces	Provide (multistructural)
Observations and measurements as evidence	Make (extended abstract)
Future motion	Predict (extended abstract)
Electric and magnetic interactions (magnets)	Determine (multistructural)
Cause and effect relationships	Ask (extended abstract) Determine (multistructural)
Objects in contact versus not in contact with each other	Ask (extended abstract) Determine (multistructural)
Simple design problem	Define (extended abstract) Solve (relational) Apply (extended abstract)

For each verb, we must read the standard to determine what level of thinking the standard expects. Does it expect learners to focus in on one relevant aspect? If so, that is unistructural. Does the verb expect students to focus on several aspects? That is multistructural. Or, does the standard expect relations and extended thinking. That would be relational and extended abstract, respectively.

Step #6 is the most important part of the unpacking process because the level of thinking dictates the expectation for students in terms of snorkeling or scuba diving. Furthermore, this significant part of the process dictates the learning progression as well as every subsequent decision about the learning experience. For the standard above, students are expected to engage in multistructural thinking and extended abstract thinking to demonstrate proficiency or mastery of this standard. This understanding of the cognitive level within the standard provides insight into the following:

1. What prior knowledge is necessary for learners to successfully engage in multistructural thinking? What learning experiences must they have to successfully build their prior learning and background knowledge? These same questions apply to extended abstract thinking? What scaffolding is necessary for all learners to successful engage in extended abstract thinking?

2. What learning experiences will encourage and engage learners at the multistructural level, relational level, or extended abstract level. How will we make thinking visible to capture student thinking? What evidence-based practices work best for these levels of thinking? How will we ensure that the evidence-based practice is really eliciting the level of thinking desired in learners?

3. How will the learning experiences promote multiple ways of interacting with the content? Cooperative learning? Small group? Whole group? What materials or manipulatives will be available to learners? What thinking strategies will be used to scaffold thinking?

Again, unpacking the standards provides a clear path forward by allowing classroom teachers to see what students **need** to know, understand, and be able to do while at the same time providing teachers the opportunity to make conscious decisions to stay the course and avoid the distractions and digressions of what is just **neat** to know, understand, and be able to do.

Do Now

Visit http://www.nextgenscience.org, and select a specific NGSS standard for a specific science content that you are preparing to teach. If your state, district, or school uses other standards besides the NGSS, select a standard that works for you. Now, repeat the process using the below template. ∎

PROGRESSION OF IDEAS, CONCEPTS, OR TOPICS (NOUNS)	DEPTH OF ENGAGEMENT (VERBS)

By completing the process of unpacking, you have extracted what learners need to know, understand, and be able to do to meet this standard, and therefore

- identified the necessary prior and background knowledge needed to successfully engage in the standard,

- mapped out a learning journey for the progression from snorkeling to scuba diving, and

- zeroed in on the cognitive levels within the standard that allow you to select the evidence-based practice that matches the level of thinking expected by the standard.

What About Bloom's Taxonomy?

As you may have noticed, the SOLO Taxonomy was used to focus on the cognitive levels within the science standards. Why not Bloom's? The mentioning of Bloom's Taxonomy often causes eyes to roll in faculty meetings. For snorkelers and scuba divers, this causes water to rush into their goggles and into their snorkels or mouthpieces leading to the sensation of drowning. However, the history and purpose of the taxonomy may help eliminate this anxiety. In the late 1950s, a group of educational psychologists headed up by Benjamin Bloom developed a classification system of cognitive behaviors valuable for designing assessments called Bloom's Taxonomy (Anderson & Sosniak, 1994; Bloom, Englehart, Furst, Hill, & Krathwohl, 1956; Krathwohl, 2002; Marzano, 2001). The cognitive levels span from the most basic of tasks like regurgitating information to the most complex cognitive activities such as evaluating information or content with a critical eye. Again, the taxonomy was designed for creating assessments, not as a progressive framework for student thinking.

Benjamin Bloom's Original Taxonomy from the most basic level to the highest, most complex level:

1. Knowledge: The student recalls or remembers information.

2. Comprehension: The student explains ideas and concepts.

3. Application: The student uses information in a different way.

4. Analysis: The student deconstructs the knowledge into different components and determines how the components relate to one another and the overall concept.

5. Synthesis: The student brings together various ideas and components and develops a comprehensive product or performance task.

6. Evaluation: The student uses the ideas and concepts to critically evaluate or take a stand for a particular viewpoint.

The particular level of Bloom's Taxonomy on which the student is working depends on the level of the question or assessment. In other words, a robust assessment would invite students to move from level to level within the same assessment.

In the early 1990s, a group of cognitive psychologists, instructional researchers, and testing and assessment specialists evaluated (ironically, the highest level of cognitive behaviors in the original Bloom's Taxonomy) the original Bloom's Taxonomy and revised it to reflect the most recent work in educational and cognitive psychology. From their work, these cognitive psychologists, headed by Lorin Anderson, one of Bloom's students, readjusted the top level of cognitive behaviors from evaluating to creating (Krathwohl, 2002; Anderson & Sosniak, 1994). In the end, they "created" the revised Bloom's Taxonomy.

Bloom's Revised Taxonomy from the most basic level to the highest, most complex level.

LEVEL OF BLOOM'S TAXONOMY		VERBS AND NOUNS ASSOCIATED WITH THE LEVEL
Remembering	Can the student recall or remember information?	define, duplicate, list, memorize, recall, repeat, reproduce, state
Understanding	Can the student explain ideas or concepts?	classify, describe, discuss, explain, identify, locate, recognize, report, select, translate, summarize
Applying	Can the student use the information in a different way?	demonstrate, illustrate, use, write, interpret, dramatize, write
Analyzing	Can the student distinguish between the different components of ideas or concepts?	appraise, compare, contrast, criticize, differentiate, discriminate, distinguish, examine, experiment, question, test
Evaluating	Can the student justify an opinion or viewpoint with the ideas or concepts?	argue, defend, judge, select, support, value, evaluate
Creating	Can the student create a new product?	assemble, construct, create, design, develop, formulate, write

SOURCE: Adapted from Blooms' Taxonomy, Vanderbilt University Center for Teaching.

Many school districts around the country, and across the globe, use Bloom's Taxonomy to make sense of the level of cognitive demand or engagement in classroom content. Although this was not the original purpose of Bloom's Taxonomy, the six levels of verbs have made a significant contribution to teachers' efforts to promote more scuba diving through questioning.

Probably the most helpful feature of "Bloom's Taxonomy 2.0" is the list of verbs associated with each level of cognitive behavior. However, solely looking at verbs and not the level of thinking (i.e., the SOLO Taxonomy) can create unexpected challenges.

Do Now

I once was in the audience during a presentation by Dr. Doug Fisher. In addition to him being an outstanding and engaging presenter, he is also a prolific writer and thinker. He asked the audience to participate in a little exercise on verbs. I would like us to replicate that exercise here.

Using Bloom's Taxonomy, where would you place the verb *list*: high, middle, or low in terms of cognitive complexity?

How about the verb *evaluate*: high, middle, or low in terms of cognitive complexity?

Odds are high that you classified the verb *list* as low in cognitive complexity and *evaluate* as high in cognitive complexity. Now, I have two questions for you:

1. On a scale from one to five, with one being terrible and five being awesome, *evaluate* the quality of your chair.

2. On a piece of scrap paper, *list* relationships between the forces that keep your chair in static equilibrium.

Do you see the problem? In this case, the level of cognitive complexity was reversed. Focusing only on verbs can be very misleading. ∎

BLOOM'S TAXONOMY AND THE SOLO TAXONOMY

With the previous exercise in mind, we should use the verbs from Bloom's Taxonomy and translate them into the SOLO Taxonomy and, finally, into classroom activities almost seamlessly. The most innovative thought leader on the implementation of the SOLO Taxonomy into classroom learning is Pam Hook (www.pamhook.com). Her work has bridged the gap between solely focusing on parts of speech, the verbs, and zeroing in on student thinking. She highlights the idea that Bloom's Taxonomy provides the verbs and the SOLO Taxonomy provides the level of thinking behind the verbs.

Do Now

Select two verbs from one of the above Bloom's Taxonomy chart. One verb should come from the remembering, understanding, or applying level while the other verb should come from the analyzing, evaluating, or creating level. Using the example for the verb *explain* from the understanding level and the two blank SOLO Taxonomy charts, describe the student responses you would expect at each level of the SOLO Taxonomy for each verb. In other words, how could the verbs *describe* or *discuss* elicit extended abstract thinking? How could the verb *support* elicit unistructural thinking? ■

VERB: *EXPLAIN*	OBSERVED LEVEL OF THINKING
Prestructural thinking	The student explains the concept using irrelevant details. From the above-unpacked example, the student might explain balanced and unbalanced forces by talking about the color or make of the toy car.
Unistructural thinking	The student explains the concept focusing on one example. The student explains balanced and unbalanced forces by describing the example provided in class or in the reading. Although relevant, it is only a single example of the phenomenon.
Multistructural thinking	The student explains the concept using several independent examples. The student can explain balanced and unbalanced forces by describing several examples but is not able to contrast the examples.
Relational thinking	The student explains the concept by comparing and contrasting several scenarios. The student can explain balanced and unbalanced forces using several examples and talking about how they are similar and different.
Extended abstract thinking	The student explains the concept by extending his or her thinking to a new or different scenario. The student explains balanced and unbalanced forces by coming up with his or her own examples and hypothesizing or predicting the relationship between the forces.

Notice that in the above example, the student is *explaining* at each level, but the depth of the thinking increases in complexity as he or she moves through the SOLO progression.

VERB: _____	OBSERVED LEVEL OF THINKING
Prestructural thinking	
Unistructural thinking	
Multistructural thinking	
Relational thinking	
Extended abstract thinking	

VERB: _____	OBSERVED LEVEL OF THINKING
Prestructural thinking	
Unistructural thinking	
Multistructural thinking	
Relational thinking	
Extended abstract thinking	

Another way of thinking about the crosswalk between Bloom's Taxonomy and the SOLO Taxonomy comes from Biggs and Collis (1982). They provided a means for assimilating verbs into the SOLO Taxonomy as a guide for the application to classroom practice. However, the same issue as in the previous Do-Now can swim up behind us if we are not careful and focus on verbs rather than thinking.

As students move more toward scuba diving, the learning experiences they are offered should incorporate higher level thinking. Student choice paired with developmentally appropriate tasks, the current level of thinking, plus one, makes for more relevant learning (Marzano, Pickering, & Heflebower, 2010). However, this brings up one remaining aspect of this first component in the framework that needs attention: Where will our students need to begin on this learning journey or progression to acquire high quality information? In other words, now that we have completed our predive preparation (i.e., unpacking the standard), identified the training needed for a successful dive (i.e., nouns and verbs), determined how deep we will go in the dive (depth of engagement), what prior and background knowledge do our divers possess? How much predive preparation will they need to be successful? Of course, we are talking about prior and background knowledge. Do we, as teachers, need to simply activate prior knowledge or build prior knowledge? How do we ensure that the divers will enter the water? Once the potential diver (learner) has entered the water, what kind of diving environment best matches students' expectations of the dive/appropriate level of difficulty? In other words, the dive environment must be at a level of difficulty just above their current level of ability (i.e., current SOLO level plus one). This is exactly where we are headed in the next chapter.

EXIT TICKET

Revisit the success criteria associated with this chapter:

1. I can explain how to unpack a science standard.

2. I can describe the balance between surface and deep learning within a science standard.

3. I can explain the relationship between unpacking a science standard, the acquisition of high quality information, and science learning progressions.

Using the following Likert scales, reflect on and evaluate your own learning:

I can explain how to unpack a science standard.

Got It　　　　　　　　　　Getting There　　　　　　　　　　Not Yet

Evidence:

I can describe the balance between surface and deep learning within a science standard.

Got It　　　　　　　　　　Getting There　　　　　　　　　　Not Yet

Evidence:

I can explain the relationship between unpacking a science standard, the acquisition of high quality information, and science learning progressions.

○――――――――――――○――――――――――――○

Got It　　　　　　　　**Getting There**　　　　　　　　**Not Yet**

Evidence:

This exit ticket encourages collaboration with colleagues to further develop and apply the ideas presented in this chapter. Set up a time to collaborate with a colleague. Together, select a science standard associated with an upcoming topic or unit. Teach the unpacking process to the colleague making sure that you articulate why this is an important process in the teaching and learning of science. Encourage your colleague to ask questions and identify gaps in your explanation. Afterward, reflect on how well you were able to teach this process to a colleague. Use the following questions to guide your reflection and discussion:

- How did you feel about your explanation?

- What did your colleague think about the process?

- Did you discover gaps in your understanding while explaining the unpacking process to your colleague?

- What would you do differently the next time?

- What are the next steps?

CHAPTER 4

Preparing for the Dive

Building and Activating Background Knowledge

Learning Intention

I understand that building and activating background knowledge in my learners is essential to surface and deep learning in the classroom.

Success Criteria

By the end of this chapter, the following success criteria will be met:

1. I can differentiate between building background knowledge and activating prior knowledge.

2. I can explain the role of checks for understanding in determining the background and prior knowledge of my learners.

3. I can create strategies that build background knowledge and activate prior knowledge in my learners.

What is the difference between building background knowledge and activating prior knowledge? How are these two concepts similar? ▪

Returning to the diver from Chapter 1, his first scuba diving experiences in Roatan, Honduras, facilitated his building of background knowledge. This background knowledge is composed of unique knowledge, skills, and understandings that he had not yet experienced but needed for a successful dive. This background knowledge, over time, becomes prior knowledge for future dives in different locations. When diving in a different location, this diver would need to activate the prior knowledge, or necessary knowledge, skills, and understandings necessary for this new dive. *Activate*, in this case, means bringing to conscious awareness.

For young learners, this distinction is exactly the same in that each individual brings to our classroom a unique set of experiences that makes up his or her background knowledge and, therefore, prior knowledge. No learner arrives as a blank slate, and to assume otherwise is simply wrong. As John Antonetti and Jim Garver highlight in their book *17,000 Classroom Visits Can't Be Wrong* (2015), students have experiences, just not our experiences.

The Big Idea

We must use prior knowledge and, at the same time, identify where additional background knowledge is needed for each learner to successfully dive into the new learning.

In the previous chapter, we engaged in the predive preparation (i.e., unpacking the standard), identified the training needed for a successful dive (i.e., nouns and verbs), and determined how deep we will go in the dive (depth of engagement). Now we explore what prior and background knowledge our divers possess.

Background and prior knowledge can be described as the essential knowledge, skills, understandings, and key experiences needed in order to successfully engage in new learning. What experiences students have or already know about the content is one of the strongest predictors of how well they will assimilate the new information (Boulanger, 1981; Alexander, Kulikowich, & Jetton, 1994, 1995; Schneider, 1993; Tobias, 1994; Pressley, Harris, & Marks, 1992; Spires & Donley, 1998; Duncan et al., 2007; La Paro & Pianta, 2000; Schuler, Funke, & Baron-Boldt, 1990; Samson, Graue, Weinstein, & Walberg, 1984). Enhancing a student's background knowledge and activating his or her prior knowledge should be a top priority when preparing to journey from snorkeler to scuba diver (Minstrell, 1989; Donovan & Bransford, 2005; Baniflower, Cohen, Pasley, & Weiss, 2008; Hattie, 2009, 2012; Bransford, Brown, & Cocking, 2000). These prior experiences are one part of the interaction between the processing and storing of information and experiences in the science classroom (Driver, Squires, Rushworth, & Wood-Robinson, 2005; Minstrell, 1989; National Science Board, 2007; Bransford et al., 2000).

Do Now

What strategies do you use to build background knowledge? What strategies do you use to activate background knowledge in your learners? Using the two-column chart below, create a list of strategies you use for each category. ▪

STRATEGIES FOR BUILDING BACKGROUND KNOWLEDGE	STRATEGIES FOR ACTIVATING BACKGROUND KNOWLEDGE

Teachers will often suggest that a lack of background and prior knowledge is one of those influential factors contributing to their student's unwillingness or inability to scuba dive. In fact, the lack of background and prior knowledge is one of the reasons learners may not even leave the shoreline, get into the boat, and ultimately jump into the water. As teachers, not only do we have to have a clear understanding of the learning progression for each and every science topic, we have to build it in the necessary background knowledge and activate what is already present in our future divers.

Next week, Ms. Showker's students will beginning learning about erosion and what changes the land, 2-ESS: Earth's Systems: Processes that Shape the Earth (NGSS Lead States, 2013). Ms. Showker and her grade-level professional learning community, or PLC, unpacked the standard last week to map out the learning progression for this particular standard. However, she now must determine the background and prior knowledge of her second graders.

2. Earth's Systems: Processes that Shape the Earth
(2-ESS1-1) Use information from several sources to provide evidence that Earth events can occur quickly or slowly.
(2-ESS2-1) Compare multiple solutions designed to slow or prevent wind or water from changing the shape of the land.

As students arrive at their science tables, they notice two plastic containers in the center of each table, one filled with sand and one filled with soil. Ms. Showker gets her students' attention and shows them what the sand and soil used to look like in the plastic containers by holding up two, untouched containers of sand and soil. She then asks them to individually complete an S-T-W (adapted from Ritchhart, Church, & Morrison, 2011).

See: What do you see? Make some observations about the containers.

Think: What does this make you think about?

Wonder: What do the containers make you wonder about? ■

BUILDING BACKGROUND KNOWLEDGE OR ACTIVATING PRIOR KNOWLEDGE? HOW DO YOU KNOW?

Ms. Showker is assessing the background and prior knowledge of her young learners. This exercise is a check for understanding that will give her a clear view of what her future scuba divers bring with them to the dive. The strategy she has selected, the S-T-W, is not as important as the information generated by the strategy.

Checking for understanding is a systematic approach used to monitor and adjust the learning journey based on student responses. Examples include entrance tickets, exit tickets, brainstorming, and student questioning. An essential component of the journey from snorkeler to scuba diver involves both the teacher and the student actively and continuously monitoring student learning through specific strategies designed to gather information on progress. This includes background and prior knowledge. In the end, checks for understanding are designed and implemented to encourage students to think about ideas, concepts, or topics in a way that makes their thinking visible.

The information generated by the checks for understanding help us, as classroom teachers, decide where to go next in the learning journey. Put differently, we are now aware of what our future scuba divers have brought to the dive and what we need to do to ensure a successful dive. Our options are (1) build background knowledge that is missing but needed for a successful dive; (2) activate prior knowledge, bringing prior experiences to conscious awareness; or (3) a combination of the two. Let's separately dive into each scenario and highlight specific strategies that get the job done.

BUILDING BACKGROUND KNOWLEDGE

Background knowledge often manifests itself as vocabulary knowledge. Thus, the academic vocabulary of our science and math students is strongly associated with the breadth and depth of their background knowledge (Marzano, 2004, 2005). In science, we recognize the importance and necessity for learners to be very comfortable with the vocabulary needed to learn the intended content within our classrooms. Take for example the difference between balanced and unbalanced forces. What is melting and freezing? What is the difference between a camouflage and mimicry? Having learners memorize the definition of the term by first copying down the definition into their notebook and then repeatedly studying the terms is not an effective way to build background knowledge. Neither are packets of worksheets. If students do not have the necessary background knowledge to comprehend the text, they may not know that they have seen organisms that mimic or use camouflage in real life.

Recent research strongly suggests that the process of building academic background knowledge should include direct vocabulary instruction (Hattie, 2009, 2012; Marzano, 2004). Direct vocabulary instruction should require students to

(1) develop descriptions of words rather than just definitions; (2) incorporate both linguistic and nonlinguistic representations; (3) include multiple exposures to the words or concepts; (4) encourage students to discuss the words or concepts; (5) require students to play with words; and (6) focus on words that are necessary for academic success (Marzano, 2004, 2005). Here are examples of what these six ideas might look like in the elementary science classroom:

CHARACTERISTICS OF DIRECT VOCABULARY INSTRUCTION	EXAMPLES
Descriptions NOT definitions	Asking learners to describe concepts, ideas, or terms; brainstorms; 3-minutes writes, and so on
Linguistic and nonlinguistic	Graphic organizers, concept maps, thinking maps, visuals, manipulatives, and so on
Multiple exposures	Working with the vocabulary through different modalities, at different times in the learning, and within different contexts
Student discussion	Think-pair-share or discussion circles
Playing with words	Analogies and metaphors
Necessary vocabulary	Terms come from the standards and are not "watered down"

 HERE'S HOW

Vocabulary Strategy #1: Beach Ball Vocabulary.

1. Get some cheap beach balls and water-based, overhead projector markers.

2. Put students into small groups of three or four students.

3. Have them select a key concept or term that is necessary for success in your science classroom.

4. Without using the concept or term, have each group write words, phrases, draw pictures, examples, or nonexamples, filling up each panel of the beach ball.

5. Have the students circle up in the room and toss the beach balls like a hot potato.

6. When time is called, each individual holding the ball picks one panel and decides what concept or term is represented by that particular panel.

(Continued)

(Continued)

Vocabulary Strategy #2: Cubing.

1. Each learner gets a template for a six-sided cube.

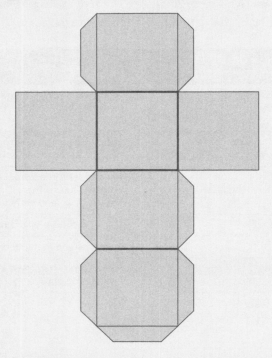

2. Learners select a vocabulary term or concept and write it on one square of the template.

3. On the other squares of the template, learners write down each one of the following terms: *Antonym*, *Synonym*, *Essential Characteristics*, and *Example*.

4. Give students time to make their cubes.

5. Once they have made their cubes, place them in a container or basket.

6. Learners, then select one from the container or basket and, as a small group or in partners, share the information about the specific term and side of the cube.

For example, if the term selected by the learner and placed on this particular cube is continental boundaries (4-ESS2-2), the student that selected this cube from the container or basket would, when it was his or her turn in the group, give an antonym or nonexample, another word or synonym for continental boundaries, describe the essential characteristics, and then give an example of a continental boundary in North America. This activity can be extended by having learners put this information into their interactive notebooks. ∎

As learners engage in this type of direct vocabulary instruction there are a number of learning benefits. The students are collaboratively developing multiple linguistic and nonlinguistic representations that will result in a deep understanding of foundational terminology for all students. The teacher could also increase student accountability by giving each group member a different color marker and expecting each member to contribute to the information on the beach ball. As the game continues, students quickly become aware that they may eventually be the ones responsible for sharing their thinking about the concepts or vocabulary terms represented on their balls with the group. Deep conceptual understanding of the concepts and terms within their unit of study is important.

Do Now

Please select a specific concept from the Next Generation Science Standards or your curriculum. Create a list of concepts, terms, and vocabulary that are necessary for a successful dive.

How will you use the characteristics of direct vocabulary instruction to help students develop a conceptual understanding of this list? Use the chart below to reflect and develop your own ideas. ■

CHARACTERISTICS OF DIRECT VOCABULARY INSTRUCTION	HOW WOULD YOU USE IT FOR YOUR LIST?
Descriptions NOT definitions	
Linguistic and nonlinguistic	
Multiple exposures	
Student discussion	

One of the many ways to encourage students to play with concepts, terms, and vocabulary is with a Word Wall. Select an area of your classroom, and designate that area as the Word Wall for a particular unit or topic. There are a couple of variations on this strategy that vary according to the amount of teacher involvement. One approach is for you, the teacher, to scatter the concepts, terms, or vocabulary all over the Word Wall. A second option would be to have students participate in a prereading or brainstorming activity where the students generate a list of concepts, terms, or vocabulary for the wall.

Ms. Taylor is trying to facilitate her students learning of vocabulary for their unit on energy (4-PS3). She calls her students' attention to a large piece of chart paper and asks them to recall words they remember from yesterday's introduction to energy. Learners used anchor charts, their interactive notebooks, and each other to generate a substantial list. After some time, Ms. Taylor began to make suggestions and add her own words to the Word Wall. To close out the activity, Ms. Taylor asks her students to alternate selecting a word from the Word Wall and explaining that word to their shoulder partners. Ms. Taylor moves around the room, eavesdropping on student conversations to assess their knowledge of the vocabulary. ■

Regardless of whether you use a teacher-generated list or a student-generated list, these words should be scattered on the Word Wall for students to see and use in context every day. As in the previous example, you might have students pick two or three words and explain their meaning to a neighbor. Students might be asked to select one or two words and create a visual sketch of the terms. As an exit activity, students might pick the concepts, terms, or vocabulary from the day's lesson and create a few sentences that conceptually link the words together. The key is to have learners interact with each other and the words on a regular basis.

To ensure multiple exposures and representations of the concepts, terms, and vocabulary necessary for academic success, learners can create a chart on which they write a description of the word (Write It), draw a visual representation of the word (Draw It), and then provide a concrete example (Apply It).

Taboo. Take the classic party game, and add a slight twist to make it a behaviorally relevant, game-like activity. Taboo is a team game where one member of the team draws a card that has a pop-culture word at the top. The goal of the person drawing the card is to get his or her teammates to guess the word at the top of the card. However, there is a catch. On the card, just below the featured word, is a list of words that cannot be used as clues. As you can probably imagine, the words on the "do not say list" are the first ones that come to mind when describing the featured word.

In the classroom, this game works the same way with one minor change. Instead of a list of words that cannot be said, students have to guess the main word and the associated words on the list.

CONCEPT, TERM, OR VOCABULARY	WRITE IT (DESCRIPTION)	DRAW IT (VISUAL)	APPLY IT (EXAMPLES)
Continental Boundaries (4-ESS2-2)	Boundaries between continents and oceans that are the locations of most volcanoes and earthquakes		Ring of Fire

Parts of a Plant	**Earth's Features**
Roots	Land
Stems	Ocean Floor
Leaves	Mountains
Colored Petals	Boundaries
Thorns	Volcanoes

The parts of the plant come from 4-LS1-1. The Earth's features list comes from 4-ESS2-2. ■

For the two examples above, learners partner up. Within those student pairs, have one student be the "talker" and one student be the "guesser." The "guesser" must try and figure out what the featured word is (i.e., parts of a plant or Earth's features) along with all of the words below the featured word.

The secret in this strategy lies in the fact that students have to talk through concepts in such a way that makes them clear to their partners. To accomplish this challenge, students must cognitively formulate a deep understanding of the concepts to effectively and efficiently articulate the ideas to their partners. If teachers select abstract concepts like balanced and unbalanced forces, students are required to construct concrete explanations, a natural progression in concept development (Willingham, 2009).

$100,000 Pyramid. This popular game show from over three decades ago provides a game-like activity for promoting conceptual understanding of science terminology. As a brief refresher of the ins and outs of this game show, let's take a trip back to the 1980s. Partners accumulated money by guessing words associated with categories on the $100,000 pyramid like "things found in a kitchen." With Dick Clark at the helm, the big prize for the winning couple was the chance to guess categories, climb up the pyramid, and take home $100,000.

The translation of this game show to the scuba diving classroom is almost seamless. Using a template of the $100,000 Pyramid, picking the categories or key ideas to go in the spaces is a natural fit.

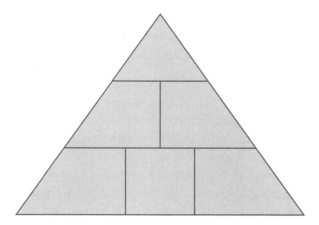

You, as the classroom teacher, can decide whether to assign point values to the various locations on the pyramid.

Examples of Categories or Concepts for the Pyramid

SCIENCE
Processes that Shape the Earth (2-ESS2)
Needs of Plants and Animals (K-LS1)
Properties of Matter (5-PS1)
Earth's Systems (5-ESS2)
Waves (1-PS4)
Fossils (3-LS4)

The previous discussion focused on preparing learners to dive into learning by ensuring they have the necessary skills, knowledge, and understandings to be successful with new learning. This background knowledge is essential for success. The previous strategies and ideas had one thing in common: They engaged students in direct vocabulary instruction that encouraged learners to (1) develop descriptions of words rather than just definitions; (2) incorporate both linguistic and nonlinguistic representations; (3) include multiple exposures to the words or concepts; (4) encourage students to discuss the words or concepts; (5) require students to play with words; and (6) focus on words that are necessary for academic success (Marzano, 2004, 2005). With this strong foundation in place, the next step is to bring prior knowledge to conscious awareness.

ACTIVATING PRIOR KNOWLEDGE

The rule of thumb for activating prior knowledge is "more of them, less of you." In other words, strategies for activating prior knowledge should require learners to dig out the information and not involve us telling them what they know. Effective strategies for activating prior knowledge include brainstorming, concept maps, knowledge maps, mind maps, turn and talks, and the classic Know-Want-Learn (KWL).

Brainstorming is a familiar strategy that can be used to encourage learners to revisit previous material and identify words, phrases, or concepts that they believe to be important and have meaning. This strategy can be done individually, with a partner, or as a group activity. For example, a teacher could arrange students into groups of three or four and provide them with a big idea or concept from a prior lesson that would be considered prior knowledge for the topic of the day. Student groups would generate their brainstorming lists as a cooperative learning task.

 HERE'S HOW

Mr. Boxley asks his students to find yesterday's work in their interactive notebooks. He then introduces the activity by reminding them that yesterday they talked about identifying materials based on their properties (5-PS1-3). Mr. Boxley then instructs his students to use their notes from yesterday to create a random word splash or develop a list of important words, phrases, or examples. "Let's see how many you can list in 3 minutes." ∎

There are many ways to engage learners in brainstorming activities. Have you ever tried to engage your entire class in a brainstorming session only to find that one or two students quickly wanted to offer many ideas within the first few seconds, while others were distracted because they needed a few minutes of processing time to think? An alternative strategy is the centerpiece strategy. Centerpiece is a brainstorming strategy that allows for flexibility in think time. As learners sit in groups, each student is given a piece of paper. There is also an extra sheet of paper in the middle of the table. When the teacher announces the topic, each student is expected to write one response on the sheet of paper in front of him or her and then exchange their sheet of paper with the one in the middle of the table. Consequently, the sheet in the middle of the table rotates on a continual basis. This allows those students who have lots of ideas to get those ideas on paper quickly while the other students have time to process their thoughts. At the end of the time given, the papers are arranged end to end providing a list of ideas from the whole group. The group members can then be given the option to cross off duplications or combine items for a more comprehensive response. Centerpiece is really a way to differentiate processing time for your students. There are many ways to add structure to a brainstorming session. In doing so, teachers will not only add individual accountability but equal participation, simultaneous interaction, and positive interdependence among the students.

Willingham and Daniel (2012) assert that one of the most effective ways to remember something is to recall it. Furthermore, the brainstorming of words, phrases, or concepts promotes the identification of critical attributes of the topic and the association of those words, phrases, or concepts with a particular big idea (Sousa, 2011). So, what else can we do with the brainstorming list? Content that is organized in a meaningful way is much easier to learn and remember than just a list of words (Durso & Coggins, 1991; Anderson, 1983).

One way to help students organize information in a meaningful way is through the creation of a mind map. These graphic organizers are visual representations of knowledge that show relationships among concepts, processes, or other ideas through connecting lines and figures (Nesbit & Adesope, 2006; Alvermann, 1981; Ives & Hoy, 2003; Winn, 1991). Ausubel (1968) believed that learners actively subsume new concepts within a conceptual framework or structure of prior knowledge (Estes, Mills, & Barron, 1969). That is, a concept map allows students to take concepts and actively organize them into a visual representation of their cognitive understanding of already existing knowledge.

Research on the instructional benefits of concept maps in instructional settings is quite positive. The use of concept maps is associated with an increase in encoding, retention, and recall (Nesbit & Adesope, 2006). From a meta-analysis of over 500 peer-reviewed studies, researchers identified a variety of uses for concept maps including individually and cooperatively generated maps from lectures or printed materials, maps as advance organizers, collaboration tools, and stand-alone collections of information (Novak & Gowin, 1984; O'Donnell, Dansereau, & Hall, 2002). Studies indicate that when concept maps are used in conjunction with text or teacher-talk, used to convert text into a visual representation, or in cooperative learning tasks and peer teaching, students demonstrated a higher level of understanding and retention of knowledge (Griffin & Robinson, 2005; Foos, 1995; and Patterson, Dansereau, & Wiegmann, 1993; Holliday, Brunner, & Donais, 1977; Horton et al., 1993). In addition, low-ability, low-background students demonstrate a greater benefit than their high-ability, high-background classmates, making the use of concept maps vital in meeting the needs of all learners (Stensvold & Wilson, 1990).

Do Now

1. Select a concept or big idea from the Next Generation Science Standards or your curriculum.

2. Brainstorm a list of words, phrases, or examples associated with your concept or big idea.

3. Create a mind map from your list, starting with a circle in the middle of the page that is about the size of an egg yolk.

4. Finally, create 3, 4, 5, or more sentences that explain the links between words, phrases, or examples in your mind map. ∎

To further encourage students' activation of prior knowledge while at the same time deepening their understanding of the knowledge is to take the mind mapping activity another step farther. Have students select several words, phrases, or examples that they have linked together and write a complete sentence that links the two words, phrases, or examples together.

A turn-to is a strategy that simply asks students to "turn to" their neighbors or folks close by and do something. That something, in this case, is talk to their neighbors about their prior knowledge. Take the brainstorming and mind mapping activity that we have developed in this chapter. Having students turn to their neighbor and explain their mind maps or read their connecting sentences offers them an opportunity to "gossip" about knowledge. As teachers engage students in these types of follow up conversations, it is often beneficial to give them advance notice of this expectation. Make them aware that after they "gossip," read, discuss, or observe a piece of information they will be expected to "say something." This response may be shared in the form of making a prediction, asking a question, clarifying something they are thinking about, or just making a simple comment. In the end, they stand a better chance of remembering it, something that is incredibly valuable for the new learning (LeDoux, 2002; Squire, 2004; Bahrick, 2000; Hasher & Zacks, 1984a; Hasher & Zacks, 1984b).

As teachers increase their use of cooperative learning and student-centered learning, it is important to structure the experience so all students are contributing to the experience and are held accountable for doing some part of the work. At the conclusion of the activity described in the example with Ms. Barnes, select several students to summarize what they learned from other members in their group.

Ms. Barnes wants to use a "stand-up, hand-up, pair-up" strategy to activate prior knowledge for today's lesson. She asks her students to grab their mind maps from yesterday, stand up, walk across the room, give someone a high five, and pair up with that person. Then, join up with another pair and arrange themselves in groups of four. She then asks her learners to number off, starting with 1, so that someone in the group is 1, someone is 2, and so on. Starting with one, each group member will take turns describing and explaining his or her mind map to the other group members. She limits each group member to approximately 2 minutes using a timer on her interactive whiteboard. Ms. Barnes walks around the room and listens in on the conversations. ■

Using a spinner, preselected playing cards, or a die, have the group member with the corresponding number stand up and share his or her summarizing thoughts. Adding this type of discussion to the end of the activity will increase the probability that students will stay on task during the group discussion from this goal-directed discussion.

For activating prior knowledge, the K-W-L Chart works as well.

K-W-L Chart

"K" – WHAT YOU ALREADY KNOW	"W" – WHAT YOU WANT TO KNOW (I.E., QUESTIONS)	"L" – WHAT YOU HAVE LEARNED

Typically, the K-W-L chart is a three-column graphic organizer that students complete by filling in the column on the far left with things they know about a particular topic, hence the *K*. The middle column is reserved for things the students want to know about that same topic, hence the *W*. Finally, the column on the far right is filled in at the end of the learning experience with things the students have learned, hence the *L*. This can be done as a class or each student can complete his or her own K-W-L chart.

As a follow up, students should place these nuggets of prior knowledge onto the class K-W-L chart. The procedure for doing this will be up to you, as the teacher, and the personality of the class. One approach is to have students share their

As students arrive to class, Ms. Brown provides each of them with a pad of sticky notes. Once they are in their seats, settling down, and curious about the sticky notes, she shows the poster-size K-W-L chart. Ms. Brown announces that the day's topic is the electrical circuit. She asks, the students what they already know about circuits. Ms. Brown prompts them to think about what they already know about circuits, to write their thoughts down on sticky notes, and stick them to their desks. Each time students think of something, they give the thought its own sticky note.

Ms. Brown wanders around the room, observing students filing out their sticky notes, offering help to those that may be stuck. ∎

nuggets by placing them on the chart one by one as they verbally share each new idea. Another approach is to have the students walk up and place their ideas on the chart as a way to get them out of their seats.

Once students have returned to their seats, have them make their own K-W-L charts and fill in the ideas that were generated on the poster-size chart. The other two columns of this graphic organizer, the *W* and the *L*, are very important as well and should be used as you move through the learning. Have your learners file away their K-W-L charts and revisit them later in the lesson on electrical circuits.

IT'S ALL IN HOW YOU ASK THE QUESTION

We often use thought-provoking questions to activate students' prior knowledge (Dantonio & Beisenherz, 2001; King, 1994). Are the questions for eliciting, probing, and extending student thinking? Do these questions seek student opinion on particular topics? Are the questions an evaluation or assessment of student understanding? Have you ever found yourself asking a student a question because a particular student was not paying attention? Teachers often use questions as a classroom management strategy to bring back the attention of a disengaged student. The reason behind asking a particular question in the classroom has a strong association with the successful activation of prior knowledge.

In general, there are two broad categories of questions: open and closed (Dohrenwend, 1965; Boaler, 1998, Allen, 2001). The most salient difference between these two broad categories of questions is the type of thinking involved in responding to an open versus a closed question. Consider the following two questions: What is the biggest impact weather has on our lives? Or, given that weather impacts our lives, what are your ideas on how to reduce the impact of weather on our lives? Semantically, the difference in these questions is subtle. Cognitively, the difference is the decision of the student to engage or not to engage. The first question is a closed question, and the second an open question. The word *biggest* closes the responses down to one acceptable answer. The exchange of these words in the second question for a phrase like *your ideas* opens the question up for multiple acceptable answers. Why is this seemingly minor difference such a big deal in the activation of prior knowledge and the willingness of your learners to get into the water?

Do Now

Reflect on the types of questions you routinely ask in your classroom. Are they open or closed questions? Jot down a few examples of the questions you ask during a science lesson. What type of responses do you get from your learners? Take a few moments, and revise your closed questions to open questions. Make a conscious effort to incorporate more open questions into your classroom. Make note of the responses from your learners. ■

Imagine for a moment that you are 8 years old and now occupy a seat in an elementary science classroom. The teacher has announced that class will begin with a review of yesterday's material. Here comes the question: "What is the most important difference between a transverse wave and a longitudinal wave?" The phrasing of this question, specifically the use of the phrase *most important*, triggers a response in the student's brain that often discourages engagement. Here is how this response goes. First, the learner must thumb through the collection of thoughts and memories associated with both transverse and longitudinal waves. This may take some time. Then the student must internally sort this collection of thoughts and memories into two mental piles, things associated with a transverse wave and things associated with longitudinal wave. After comparing and contrasting these two mental heaps and making a mental list of their differences, the learner must select the *most important* one. Up until this point, the student is more than likely cognitively engaged as he or she completes the above mental tasks. However, one final step is left in processing a response to this seemingly harmless question for activating prior knowledge. The student must ask himself or herself, "Is the most important difference on my list the same as the most important difference on the teacher's list?" To avoid being wrong and saving face with his or her peers, the student will probably not respond or not volunteer to engage in this activation of prior knowledge all because the teacher asked a closed question. When asking a closed question, the teacher is subconsciously signaling to the students that only one response will qualify as an acceptable response and thus requires convergent thinking. Convergent thinking is associated with the development of a single answer with no room for ambiguity (Runco & Acar, 2012). For students developing an understanding of a concept in science, this can be disengaging (Allen, 2001).

On the flip side of the scenario described above, adjusting this question about mechanical waves to a more open question eliminates this internal tug-of-war with the brain and student engagement. What if the teacher had first asked students to brainstorm a list of characteristics or features associated with transverse waves and then, after some time, asked students to brainstorm a separate list of characteristics or features associated with longitudinal waves? As open questions, these two tasks encourage divergent thinking, which subconsciously signals to students that there is a collection of responses that qualify as acceptable responses. Divergent thinking is associated with creative thinking and the opportunity to explore a variety of outcomes (Runco & Acar, 2012). For students developing an understanding of a concept in science, this approach provides a safe environment for them to explore and share their thinking without the fear of not selecting the single correct or acceptable answer. This is safer and more engaging (Allen, 2001)! From a teacher's perspective, the level of student responding will go up simply because it is a safer activation of prior knowledge that encourages a variety of responses.

The acquisition of high quality information, the first component of our instructional framework, depends on two main things: identifying what learners need to know and the necessary background and prior knowledge needed to be successful. Once the potential diver (learner) has entered the water, focusing on the necessary knowledge, skills, and understandings need for the journey from snorkeler to scuba diver allows us to determine what kind of diving environment best matches students' expectations of the dive/appropriate level of difficulty. Next, we move to the second component of the instructional framework, which focuses on the diving environment.

EXIT TICKET

Revisit the success criteria associated with this chapter:

1. I can differentiate between building background knowledge and activating prior knowledge.

2. I can explain the role of checks for understanding in determining the background and prior knowledge of my learners.

3. I can create strategies that build background knowledge and activate prior knowledge in my learners.

Using the following Likert scales, reflect on and evaluate your own learning:

I can differentiate between building background knowledge and activating prior knowledge.

Got It   Getting There   Not Yet

Evidence:

I can explain the role of checks for understanding in determining the background and prior knowledge of my learners.

Got It   Getting There   Not Yet

Evidence:

I can create strategies that build background knowledge and activate prior knowledge in my learners.

Got It   Getting There   Not Yet

Evidence:

The following exit ticket is a model for assessing student understanding of key concepts and vocabulary. For the purposes of modeling, complete the exit ticket below using the concept Background and Prior Knowledge. On a scale of 1 to 4, with 4 being the highest, how would you rate your understanding of the importance of background knowledge and prior knowledge in the progression from snorkeling to scuba diving? In your own words, write a summary of the importance of background and prior knowledge. Finally, develop a visual representation of the terms, *background knowledge or prior knowledge*, and list examples for developing background knowledge and activating prior knowledge.

EXIT TICKET

Concept: Background Knowledge **My Understanding: 1 2 3 4**

Summary: _____

_____

_____

_____

_____

_____

Drawing: **More Ideas:**

CHAPTER 5

From Snorkelers to Scuba Divers

Picking the Diving Environment, Step #2—Evidence-Based Models of Instruction

Learning Intention

I understand that the selection of the appropriate learning environment can have a significant impact on the effectiveness of instruction and learning.

Success Criteria

By the end of this chapter, the following success criteria will be met:

1. I can describe three different models of instruction.

2. I can identify the attributes of direct instruction, inquiry-based instruction, and cooperative learning.

3. I can align the learning environment with the appropriate method of instruction.

PICKING THE DIVING ENVIRONMENT

Let's come up for air and switch the metaphor for a moment. Imagine for a moment that you are hungry and, with a companion, in search of a place to eat. Let's imagine that you just walked into a famous local restaurant, known for the quality of their menu as well as the quantity of options on the menu. The hostess quickly walks you and your guest over to a corner booth and hands you one of their rather elaborate menus. How do you read and review menus? What are the thoughts and questions going through your mind? Do these thoughts and questions vary depending on how hungry you are? Really, think about this for a moment. How do you read and review a menu at a restaurant that you are visiting for the very first time? Your questions might include the following: What am I in the mood to eat? How much money do I have to spend? Should I order something that I recognize or have had elsewhere? Again, does this vary depending on your level of hunger? For some individuals, these decisions are purposeful, intentional, and deliberate based on how they want their next meal to "go together." Others may allow the choices of their companion, a neighboring table, or the advertised special on the sign by the door influence their decision.

Now bridge this analogy to your instructional decisions. How do you select your approach to teaching and learning in your own classroom? Within education, there are numerous models of instruction that can be implemented in any classroom, on any day of the week, for just about any content. For example, are you going to use direct instruction, vocabulary acquisition, concept attainment, inquiry-based learning, problem-based learning, or project-based learning? Like ordering from a menu, similar thinking goes into our decisions about selecting the model of instruction from the menu of options available to us in our classrooms. Do we select our model of instruction based on our mood or what would be fun? Do I have the supplies to teach the content using this model (i.e., the money question)? Am I picking a model with which I am most comfortable? Or, do we select the model of instruction because it aligns with the main course for the day: the content knowledge and process skills represented within our learning intention and success criteria? Clearly, the last question is the correct way of approaching this decision and is the focus of this chapter.

As you select and prepare your learning environment what are the important things you really need to consider? Even though you may have taught this content many times there are always unique factors that influence your instructional practices. Taking this analogy to snorkeling and scuba diving, this is selecting the appropriate dive location. Every decision is affected by the water quality, the individuals who are diving with you, the time of year, as well as what the diver wants to learn and observe. If we really want deep-focused and amazing discoveries, there are multiple things to consider. The captain of the boat, the diving guide, is responsible for picking the location and monitoring the dive.

The starting point for selecting the diving environment is the combination of clear learning intentions and success criteria, awareness of each learner's prior knowledge and background knowledge, and focusing on what students need to know and not what is neat to know. These components were explained and developed in a previous chapter and are essential when identifying the most appropriate and effective model of instruction.

Do Now

Predict and describe the relationship between learning intentions, success criteria, and model of instruction. Summarize your thinking here. ∎

_____

_____

_____

_____

Selecting a diving environment that does not align with the learning intention or success criteria for the day will yield learner confusion, disengagement, and barriers to learners meeting the expectations articulated in the learning intention and success criteria. If the diving environment requires content knowledge and process skills not yet acquired by the learners, or the environment is not challenging enough, learners will disengage and be hesitant to engage in future dives. Finally, if the diving environment does not support learners focusing on what they need to know without being distracted by things that are neat to know, learning will suffer from this distraction.

DIVING ENVIRONMENTS—MODELS OF INSTRUCTION

Let's explore three specific models of instruction that range from a predominantly teacher-directed model to more student-directed approaches. In other words, the model progresses toward the gradual release by the captain of the boat or the diving guide allowing more diver-directed exploration. However, regardless of the level of release, each model of instruction is designed to be purposefully selected and implemented based on the desired learning outcomes of the classroom teacher. Otherwise, we are just randomly ordering food that we may or may not like or dropping divers into an area of water that is not conducive to diving because of lack of items to explore or outright danger. Like diving, danger in the classroom is never good!

The Big Idea

We must ensure that our approach to instruction matches the type of thinking we are striving for in our learners.

Do Now

Tap into your prior knowledge regarding models of instruction. Using a Likert scale (1-5), what do you believe is your current level of knowledge about each of the three models? The second column asks you to think about when you would use each particular method of instruction.

Finally, as you think about each method of instruction, take a moment to identify what you believe are the benefits and challenges associated with each model. ■

MODEL OF INSTRUCTION	LEVEL OF KNOWLEDGE NEEDED TO ENGAGE IN THE MODEL (1 LOW-5 HIGH)	PURPOSE FOR SELECTING THE MODEL (E.G., WHAT TYPE OF LEARNING IS EXPECTED IN WITH THE MODEL?)	BENEFITS AND CHALLENGES
Direct instruction			
Inquiry-based instruction			
Cooperative learning			

All models of instruction are appropriate and adaptable for engaging all students but only when used for types of learning. In other words, no one approach works all of the time. And, whether an approach works some of the time depends on when the approach is used in science learning. For example, inquiry-based instruction may not be the ideal choice if learners do not have the prior content knowledge or process skills to effectively and efficiently inquire about a topic. Although we could unpack each and every model of instruction in the educational literature (see Estes & Mintz, 2015), the sheer volume would distract from the point of this component in the framework. Just like picking the ideal diving environment for an anxious group of divers, it takes smart teaching habits to effectively select and implement the correct method of instruction for learners.

DIRECT INSTRUCTION

When implemented correctly, direct instruction is unparalleled in its ability to improve student learning outcomes. Direct instruction has a bad reputation, often used synonymously with "sit and get" or lecture. Yet, research has continued to find that direct instruction is a highly effective method of instruction (Adams & Englemann, 1996; Fischer & Tarver, 1997; Forness, Kavale, Blum, & Lloyd, 1997), producing greater learning outcomes beyond other instructional approaches such as discovery learning or problem-based learning (see Klahr and Nigam, 2004). Direct instruction has been used in a variety of contexts from inner-city to rural schools, as well as with learners from a variety of backgrounds. There is a wide range of examples where direct instruction is associated with significant learning outcomes (Adams & Englemann, 1996; Fischer & Tarver, 1997; Forness et al., 1997).

Direct instruction is a highly scripted and structured method that, when used effectively, is rich in rigorous content. Direct instruction involves (1) activating prior knowledge; (2) explicitly teaching new content; (3) providing opportunities for guided practice; (4) using the guided practice to provide corrective feedback; and (5) providing independent practice (Estes & Mintz, 2015). As with any instructional model, the direct instruction approach is based on clear learning intentions, success criteria, and consideration of learners prior or background knowledge. Direct instruction does not only use lecture, or "sit and get," but uses evidence-based strategies during the presentation of new material, guided practice sessions, and independent practice (e.g., visuals, graphic organizers, classroom discussion, etc.). Strategies discussed in the previous chapter on prior and background knowledge are far from "sit and get." And, in the upcoming chapters, there are additional strategies for the other parts of direct instruction.

Do Now

Consider the steps in direct instruction. What strategies do you use or would consider using for each step? ∎

STEPS IN DIRECT INSTRUCTION	POTENTIAL STRATEGIES OR STRATEGIES I USE
Activating prior knowledge or review	
Explicit teaching of new content	
Guided practice	
Corrective feedback	
Independent practice	

So why would and should a teacher select direct instruction for the diving environment? Building strong content knowledge and process skills is essential for later learning. Direct instruction provides a framework for building that knowledge and those skills. Again, the key to successful learning is to match the method of instruction to the learning intention and success criteria. For example, if you want students to learn the eight planets in the order of the distance from the sun, this is done most effectively and efficiently through direct instruction. However, if you want students to learn about the factors that contribute to an object sinking or floating in water, direct instruction may not provide the level of engagement needed for this learning.

Do Now

Peruse your standards and science curriculum. When looking at the standards, what content knowledge and process skills appear to be best learned through direct instruction?

When you find these topics in your curriculum, how are they suggested to be taught or learned? After reading this far into the book, do you agree or disagree? Why? ∎

Returning to the diving analogy, breathing underwater for the first time is something that you will never forget. Yet there are specific things that a diver must learn before he or she is able to safely and successfully experience that joy. Although many dive shops provide you with the basic gear as you learn including a mask, snorkel, fins, regulator, buoyancy control device, dive gauges, and a tank, you still need direct instruction on how to properly use this equipment. Diving into the water and learning to use the equipment through inquiry or cooperative learning would be dangerous. All divers begin under the direct guidance of a professional: reviewing, explicit teaching, guided practice, corrective feedback, and, only then, independent practice. Most divers bring prior and adequate swimming skills. However, you will not find any instructor who will take you out in the boat and just throw you in the water.

 HERE'S HOW

> **3. Inheritance and Variation of Traits: Life Cycles and Traits**
>
> (3-LS1-1) Develop models to describe that organisms have unique and diverse life cycles but all have in common birth, growth, reproduction, and death.

Ms. Butler wants her students to learn that the changes plants go through, the life cycle of a plant, form a pattern. In order for students to be successful, Ms. Butler decided that her students needed to have a firm understanding of the process of germination. Germination is foundational content knowledge for this particular learning intention.

Ms. Butler begins by gathering her students on the carpet. As the students sit down in a circle, she places several seeds on the carpet in front of them. In order to stimulate their cognitive thinking and activate their prior knowledge, she tells the learners that she is going to begin by reading the book, *The Tiny Seed*, by Eric Carle. She tells the learners to observe the seeds and think about the following questions:

What would I see if I cut the seed in half?

How do seeds travel?

Where did this seed come from?

After reading the story, Ms. Butler engages the class in a brief conversation by using guided questioning. What happened to the tiny seed? What blows the seeds around? Did the tiny seed grow? She extends the conversation by asking her learners what they could have done to help the tiny seed grow. What is the purpose of the flower losing its seeds? She wraps up the discussion by asking them, what they think they would see if she cut some of the seeds in half?

Ms. Butler explicitly teaches her students that seeds play a very important role in the reproduction of plants. "Seeds come in different shapes and sizes, just like the ones on our carpet. Seeds have their own parts, just like other living things. Today, you are going to learn the different parts of a seed." At this point, Ms. Butler projects an illustration of a seed on the whiteboard with the word *germination* in big bold letters.

(Continued)

(Continued)

Referring back to one of the previous student responses, she tells the class that Samuel thought that if he cut open the seed he would find a plant. "Germination actually is the process by which plants emerge from a seed and begin to grow." This illustration shows the parts of the seed during germination. Ms. Butler continues to identify, define, and describe the embryo, radicle, seed coat, and cotyledons.

After this explicit teaching of new content, Ms. Butler hands each student index cards. Each card identifies one part of the seed on one side of the card and the definition or description on the other side of the card.

Embryo: A very young plant from which a new plant grows given the proper conditions.

Radicle: The first part of the seed to grow that develops into the primary root.

Cotyledons: The part of the embryo within the seed that becomes the first leaves.

Seed Coat: The outer protective covering of the seed.

In order to provide each student an oral rehearsal of these terms, she uses the index cards to engage the students in an activity called Quiz-Quiz-Trade. The class has experienced this activity before so they know when the music begins that the students are to walk around the room until the music stops at which time they find partners. The students quiz each other on their particular seed part. Due to the fact that this is early in the learning process, students will likely use the information on the back of the card for support and clarification (guided practice with corrective feedback). After that exchange, the partners switch cards. The music begins, and the process is repeated.

To conclude the lesson, learners are given an exit ticket (independent practice) where they are asked to identify the parts of a seed and to describe the parts. ∎

Do Now

As you reflect on the next science unit or lesson you plan for your learners, are you able to identify the parts of the content knowledge and process skills that are foundational and need to be directly taught? Spend a few minutes and revisit your responses to the previous Do-Now. Do you still agree with what would or would not be best learned through direct instruction? Furthermore, ask yourself, how am I going to ensure the topics best learned through direct instruction are not restricted to "sit and get" learning? ∎

INQUIRY-BASED INSTRUCTION

Just as divers cannot be asked to learn certain content knowledge and process skills on their own, learners absolutely cannot understand the immensity of the sea by sitting on the beach. After learners have the necessary prior knowledge and background knowledge, it is time to offer them opportunities to engage in learning that is less teacher directed and more student led. Have you ever heard the statement, "tell me and I forget, show me and I remember, involve me and I understand"? This statement implies that active engagement leads to better understanding. This could very well be the mantra behind inquiry-based instruction. Inquiry-based instruction is a method whereby students explore concepts for themselves through the use of carefully set up learning experiences. Although children are born with a sense of curiosity and exploration, along the way classroom practices have stifled student's inquisitiveness. As you may recall from the first chapter of this book, young learners perceive, quite quickly, that teachers are looking for the right answers (Medina, 2014a). Thus, curiosity as an innate feature of the brain, at least in classroom learning, is extinguished. Again, most of the talking in classrooms is teacher directed and focused on factual knowledge, giving students 1 second or less to think and respond (Cazden, 2001). Within the educational process, there is definitely a place for right answers, but this method of instruction promotes a greater understanding of *how*. *How* things change, *how* concepts are interrelated, and *how* ideas are organized, using relevant authentic situations that people face throughout their lives.

Do Now

Peruse your standards and science curriculum, again. When looking at the standards, what content knowledge and process skills appear to be best learned through inquiry? When you find these topics in your curriculum, how are they suggested to be taught or learned? Do these standards also contain content knowledge and process skills that are best aligned for direct instruction? Is there a trend emerging? ∎

Inquiry-based instruction involves (1) the hook; (2) formulation of questions; (3) selecting a question; (4) peer collaboration; (5) answering the question; (6) sharing findings; and (7) evaluation and assessment. Important instructional decisions need to be made at each step to initiate a successful inquiry-based learning experience. What relevant hook are you going to offer to stimulate and motivate learning? How will you trigger learners' curiosity? Is it a matter of activating prior knowledge or perhaps you need to spend a few minutes building background knowledge? How are you going to help students discover the questions they will be expected to answer? As you examine these questions, it becomes very apparent that the role of the teacher is quite different within this model of instruction. The answer to these questions initially engages students or gives the potential diver a relevant purpose or excuse to leave the beach or boat and get into the water. No one would ever deny the importance of knowing your students. Effective teachers know their students and use this knowledge to adapt or optimize their instruction with timely interventions during the learning process when misconceptions appear. The importance of monitoring student learning should never be underestimated.

Inquiry-based instruction is a conscious decision that your students are ready to explore the content with an increased level of independence. Learning needs to be fostered and supported but not controlled or dictated in the same structured

Do Now

On March 12th, we moved our clocks one hour ahead overnight, and daylight savings time began. The following morning, while visiting an elementary school, Olivia, a fifth-grade student, approached her teacher as she entered the classroom and began to ask questions about daylight saving time. What does daylight saving time really do? Does it really save us time? Does it give us extra time? As she continued to ask questions, it quickly occurred to the teacher that her mind was flooded with ideas, and her level of curiosity was high. This was a great opportunity for exploration. Olivia's final question was, "do we really need daylight saving time?"

Use this scenario to think about inquiry-based instruction. Would you use inquiry-based instruction to help answer Olivia's questions? Spend some time thinking through the conscious decisions a teacher would need to make in order to make this a productive learning experience.

- What prior knowledge would you want to uncover?
- What background knowledge is needed for successful exploration?
- What essential questions would stimulate curiosity?
- What experience and strategies would you use to engage her and other students?
- Is this the method of instruction you would have selected to teach your students?
- If not, describe the instruction you would have implemented. ∎

fashion of direct instruction. As teachers front-load the experience with relevant hooks, stimulate curiosity with authentic engaging scenarios, and check students' level of understanding, teachers become confident that with the use of essential questions, students will dive in and explore the learning. Be careful, there are divers who might think, "who needs all that cumbersome equipment, snorkeling seems good enough." The teacher must remain vigilant to ensure that the environment includes support and guidance, stocked with resources, strategies, and materials.

Did these questions take you out of your comfort zone? A scuba diver is safe in his or her dive boat, but that is not the best use of the dive equipment. Teachers often step out of their comfort zone as they step into the world of inquiry-based instruction. As teachers and learners engage in inquiry-based instruction and learning, there are both gems and opportunities in this model of instruction.

Classroom teachers may feel that inquiry-based instruction is easier to use because the learning process is handed off to the students. Students are often very excited to dive into the task or get started with the investigation. Together, these two reactions make inquiry-based instruction a popular choice regardless of the type of learning. As with direct instruction, inquiry-based instruction requires purposeful and intentional decision making on the part of the teacher so that learners have clear parameters for their own intentional and purposeful decision making during the inquiry experience. Although subtle, this difference is important. Inquiry-based instruction must be set up so that it not only aligns with the types of learning, but also the inquiry experience must be structured so that learners have the prior knowledge, background knowledge, and resources to make intentional and purposeful decisions. Otherwise, lessons will be met with "I don't know" or "can you just tell us the answer?"

 HERE'S HOW

5. Structure and Properties of Matter
(5-PS1-3) Make observations and measurements to identify materials based on their properties.

Mr. Knod has launched his learners into a learning experience confident that he has spent time activating his students' prior knowledge and developing their background knowledge, where necessary. Students must know key vocabulary and enter with some basic knowledge about the physical properties of minerals. Mr. Knod is well aware that during this activity, vocabulary may need to be revisited and clarified. To start, the students are put into groups of four. Mr. Knod asks the

(Continued)

(Continued)

person "who woke up the latest this morning" to come get the necessary supplies. Within the bag are the following items: a glass plate, various types of minerals, a streak plate, and a magnifying glass. With little input from the teacher, each team is directed to examine and discuss everything they know about the materials provided in their supply baskets.

Upon completion of their discussion, Mr. Knod walks around the room giving each group a bag. As he distributes these bags, he offers the entire group this scenario: Due to your vast knowledge about rocks and minerals, you are now employed by our local museum. As you return to work after your lunch break, the head custodian hands you a mineral and tells you he found it on the floor. That mineral is in the bag I just gave you. It does not have a label. Your team must explain what process you would go through to correctly identify that mineral. Use what you already know about the properties of minerals.

Before the students get started, Mr. Knod continues to communicate the learning intention and success criteria. He informs students that he will be using a rubric to ensure collaborative group work to perform the investigation, that students are using the physical properties to identify the mineral, and that their explanations have to include the key vocabulary that was addressed during the direct instruction portion of this unit. ▪

No matter what method of instructional delivery you decide to use, closure is an effective research-based strategy. It is important to bring the students back together to report their findings and summarize their learning(s), not only to the teacher but also to each other. This is a great opportunity to check for understanding by asking thought-provoking questions. For example, what discoveries did you make while you were in the process of identifying your mineral? What problems did you run into while trying to identify the mineral, and how did you address those issues?

Do Now

Develop a list of closure activities that provide learners the opportunity to summarize their learning and link their learning directly to the learning intention and success criteria. ▪

One of the outcomes of inquiry-based instruction is discovery of useful knowledge. When what the content learners are learning is perceived as useful, meaningful, and relevant to students, they will often accept the level of challenge and put forth the effort needed to complete the task. Inquiry often leads to a greater understanding of the world in which students live, learn, communicate, and work.

Many would say that the success of inquiry-based instruction is a teacher's ability to stimulate curiosity and ask the right questions while students are engaged in the learning. Triggering curiosity is no small feat. Some teachers become so focused on modeling enthusiasm and setting the stage for a deep level of inquisitiveness that they put the students to work without that strong conceptual foundation needed in order to develop meaningful connections and deeper levels of cognitive engagement. Although inquiry-based learning allows students to investigate and explore, teachers need to remember that inquiry is a continuum of exploration. A teacher-directed task might ask students to confirm an idea that is already known in advance, or it may be in the form of a teacher-presented question where the students are asked to use a set of prescribed procedures. We may decide to move away from teacher-directed tasks and ask students to investigate using student-designed questions and procedures. Educators use all levels of inquiry that move students away from teacher-directed exploration into a world of student-centered thinking and learning. No matter where you are on the continuum, it is imperative that you set your students up for success with the adequate knowledge and skills.

COOPERATIVE LEARNING

Learning is a social activity. Opportunities to discuss learning, exchange ideas, challenge or question ideas, and reason through science concepts are essential to learning (Zembal-Saul, McNeill, & Hershberger, 2012). How much time do you spend making conscious decisions about the interactions that will occur within your classroom? How teachers structure the interaction between themselves to students, student to student, or even student to material is an essential component within the planning process. Educators continue to hear about the importance of developing, what is commonly called, the "21st Century" skills within our students. Over and over you hear that today's students are entering a workforce that demands proficiency in skills associated with communication, collaboration, critical thinking, initiative, metacognition, persistence, and even synergy.

David Johnson and Roger Johnson (1999) identified five basic elements that allow successful small-group learning: positive interdependence, face-to-face interaction, individual and group accountability, group behaviors, and group processing. This triggered a shift in the roles of teachers and students. It also stimulated multiple challenges and questions. In 2001, *Classroom Instruction that Works* cited research showing that cooperative learning can lead to student achievement gains as high as 28 percentiles (Marzano, Pickering, & Pollock, 2001). Just like scuba diving, you can't just throw a teacher into a classroom and tell him or her to do cooperative learning. Cooperative learning or group work may sound easy, but, often times, the skills necessary to be a collaborative team player require a structured learning environment.

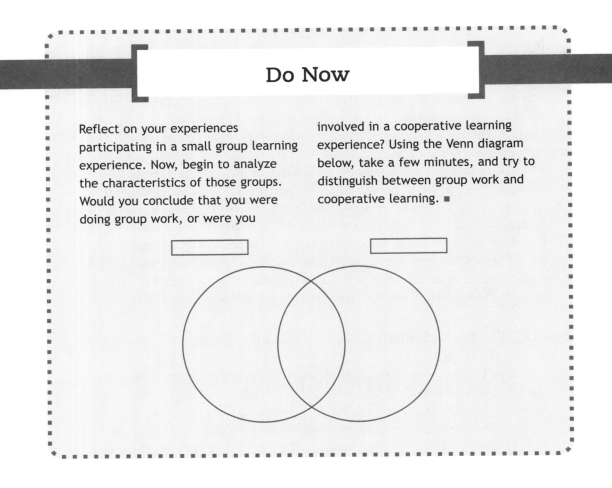

Do Now

Reflect on your experiences participating in a small group learning experience. Now, begin to analyze the characteristics of those groups. Would you conclude that you were doing group work, or were you involved in a cooperative learning experience? Using the Venn diagram below, take a few minutes, and try to distinguish between group work and cooperative learning. ■

How often have you put students into groups and spent hours designing a highly engaging learning experience only to have one or maybe two students in the group do all the work. It's totally unintentional, but most of the time there is a student who loves taking the lead and often does so on the assigned task or activity. This is typically an attribute of group work versus cooperative learning. Holding students individually accountable is not an easy task, but it is the key attribute of cooperative learning. Kagan Cooperative Learning Structures (Kagan, 1989) provide structures for positive interdependence, face-to-face interaction, individual and group accountability, group behaviors, and group processing.

One of the authors of this book is reminded of the Christmas she woke up, and her children surprised her with an electric drill. She was so excited. Surprisingly, that is exactly what she had asked for from Santa Claus. As she unwrapped the gift and discovered what she had received, she ran around the house looking for somewhere to use this new electric drill. Often, that is exactly how teachers behave when it comes to group work or cooperative learning. Teachers immediately try to think about where they can plug in the drill or use cooperative learning. Teachers should focus on the learning target and what they want to happen in the minds of their learners, and only then should they identify the right tool or cooperative learning strategy to successfully get that job done. What mindset do you have as you make conscious decisions about your use of cooperative learning?

Do Now

Peruse your standards and science curriculum one last time. When looking at the standards, what content knowledge and process skills appear to be best learned through cooperative learning or social interaction? When you find these topics in your curriculum, how are they suggested to be taught or learned? Do these standards also contain content knowledge and process skills that are best aligned for direct instruction or inquiry-based instruction? How could either of those two models include cooperative learning? ■

Kagan Cooperative Strategies (1989) are categorized and designed with purpose in mind. These structures support and aide a teacher's decision-making process. Do I need a structure that requires students to think about specific content in a specific way? Maybe during this learning experience students must engage in the communication of ideas (e.g., explain, discuss, or give evidence). In this case, the selection process would focus on a structure that would promote communication or analyzing and processing information. Again, effective science instruction depends on finding the right tool for the content knowledge and process skills. An effective teacher is able to identify what should be going on in the minds of their learners and embed a cooperative learning strategy that promotes that type of learning.

Mr. Howes, a second-grade teacher at Pebble Elementary School, is giving a science quiz tomorrow and is concerned about the level of mastery with the concepts students are expected to learn. His students spent about a week learning and exploring the properties of matter. Within this unit, there was an expectation that students would understand the difference between reversible and irreversible change as it relates to the heating and cooling process.

2. Structure and Properties of Matter
(2-PS1-4) Construct an argument with evidence that some changes caused by heating or cooling can be reversed and some cannot.

Mr. Howes designed an activity that will not only review some of the important vocabulary but will also have the students communicate their understanding of the concepts taught to each other, hold all students accountable for thinking and listening, and open the door to strong collaboration among classmates. Mr. Howes decided to engage his students using a strategy called, "Numbered Heads Together." Like other Kagan Cooperative Structures (1989), this strategy can be used within any content area, but at this point, Mr. Howes selected this specific strategy to review these specific science concepts.

After putting the students in groups of four, he has each group count off by 4. When each student has a number, Mr. Howes explains that he will pose a question or a statement to the entire group, and each group must pick their "butts" up and put their "heads" together and decide on a response.

He puts the first statement up on the smart board:

- Provide an example of an object or a material that is changed when heated but can be reversed as the same object or material is cooled again.

Each group is given several minutes to discuss their group response. Mr. Howes uses a Kagan group spinner and announces a particular group number. Each student with the same number stands and shares their group response. The teacher facilitates the conversation in order to ensure student understanding and to address any misconceptions. Notice the engagement power within the strategy. During the group conversations, all students are held accountable to at least listen. If there is a student who is unaware of the correct response, he or she will pay attention enough to repeat the response just in case his or her number is called on. Each standing student is expected to take it one step further and is asked to repeat or summarize the group discussion. Individual accountability, simultaneous interaction, and positive interaction are powerful learning components that enhance the effectiveness of cooperative learning. Mr. Howes continues with rigorous questions designed to engage students behaviorally, cognitively, and emotionally. ∎

Do Now

Locate a science lesson that you will be using in your classroom. Analyze the levels of cooperative engagement within that particular lesson. Take the time to make some specific adjustments in order to increase the levels of

- individual accountability,
- equal participation,
- simultaneous interaction, and
- positive team interaction. ■

THE ESSENTIAL ROLE OF THE TEACHER, THE VIEW FROM THE BOAT

We must never forget the essential role of the teacher. Just like the captain in the boat, supervision is not only mandatory, but the leadership and the lead line gives the divers a sense of security and a feeling of safety. The captain often has information that is out of the perspective of the individual divers but valuable to the diving experience. Just like in the classroom, the boat captain who takes people diving all of the time has the ability to describe each diving experience at certain times of the year adding specific details about each diving location, as well as offering suggestions about the certain times of the day (night versus day diving) that promote the best opportunity for transfer of knowledge. Teachers are continually offering ideas and knowledge, asking questions, focusing attention on specifics that are relevant, providing meaningful connections, reorganizing, and providing elaborate rehearsal of content.

As teachers monitor and adjust the learning experience, it provides the students with a sense that "my teacher cares and will not let me fail." The instructional approaches a teacher uses can make or break the entire learning experience. Selecting an ineffective method of instruction can also result in learner confusion, disengagement, and barriers to learners meeting the expectations articulated in the learning intention and success criteria. Learners will often disengage and become hesitant to engage in the future.

The teacher's level of knowledge about the participants will not only enhance but also have a tremendous impact on the outcomes of any learning experience. The captain of a dive boat will be the first to tell you, in order to do the best job possible, you need to know exactly who is in your boat. Many dive captains would say that knowing and gathering information about the divers in their boat is absolutely essential. Being aware of their prior knowledge, level of confidence, and previous diving experiences can significantly impact the decisions being made about the diving location and the degree of challenge and support, as well as the depth and length of the dive. This is analogous to differentiating the instruction in your classroom. Meeting your students where they are and taking them one step beyond their comfort zone will provide the appropriate level of challenge and rigor. Teachers often reflect on (1) if the learners are ready for individual exploration; (2) if they need additional guided practice; or (3) if they are in need of additional background knowledge. As teachers develop the appropriate learning environment, aligned with the most effective method of instruction, they are continually making conscious decisions before, during, and after instruction that ultimately increase the probability that students will learn.

EXIT TICKET

Revisit the success criteria associated with this chapter.

1. I can describe three different models of instruction.

2. I can identify the attributes of direct instruction, inquiry-based instruction, and cooperative learning.

3. I can align the learning environment with the appropriate method of instruction.

Using the following Likert scales, reflect on and evaluate your own learning:

I can describe three different models of instruction.

Got It   Getting There   Not Yet

Evidence:

I can identify the attributes of direct instruction, inquiry-based instruction, and cooperative learning.

Got It   Getting There   Not Yet

Evidence:

I can align the learning environment with the appropriate method of instruction.

Got It   Getting There   Not Yet

Evidence:

EXIT TICKET

As you reflect on Chapter 5, complete the following circle, square, triangle activity.

Circle/Square/ Triangle.

Write down something that is circling around in your brain, (or questions you have).

(*Continued*)

Jot down something you heard that squared with your thinking, (or something you agree with).

Explain something that you are seeing or understanding from a different angle, (or important points you want to remember).

CHAPTER 6

Navigating the Diving Environment

Evidence-Based Strategies

Learning Intention

I understand that that the specific teaching and learning strategies I select strongly influence the learning outcomes of my learners.

Success Criteria

By the end of this chapter, the following success criteria will be met:

1. I can compare and contrast the different types of engagement in the science classroom.

2. I can explain the relationship between student engagement and the selection of teaching and learning strategies.

3. I can match specific teaching and learning strategies with the level of engagement I expect in learners.

The divers are in the water! We have arrived at this place in the fostering and nurturing learner interest and engagement in K–5 science that results in higher-order thinking and deep conceptual understanding by

1. developing the learning progression for learners to journey from snorkeler to scuba diver using the SOLO Taxonomy;

2. identifying what divers need to know, understand, and be able to do through unpacking the standards;

3. using prior knowledge and, at the same time, identifying where additional background knowledge is needed for each learner to successfully dive into the new learning; and

4. selecting the ideal diving environment by identifying the model of instruction that best matches the desired learning outcomes.

Do Now

Pause for a moment and retrieve the big ideas and details associated with each of the above four statements. Try and do this without looking back into the previous chapters. The graphic organizer can help organize your thoughts. What do you remember? After you have devoted some time to the below chart, look back through the previous chapters, and fill in any gaps in your learning. ■

WHAT I REMEMBER
Developing the learning progression for learners to journey from snorkeler to scuba diver using the SOLO Taxonomy
Identifying what divers need to know, understand, and be able to do through unpacking the standards
Using prior knowledge and, at the same time, identifying where additional background knowledge is needed for each learner to successfully dive into the new learning
Selecting the ideal diving environment by identifying the model of instruction that best matches the desired learning outcomes

Each diving guide, having selected the ideal diving environment, with his or her lead line and navigational equipment on the boat, carefully watches from above aiming for each diver to engage in the carefully selected diving environment. The goal is for divers to safely and effectively take in the aquatic ecosystem around them and meet their every expectation of the day. In addition, each diving guide strives for their divers to want more. As first mentioned in the Introduction, this is the difference between *diversive* and *epistemic curiosity*. A well selected diving environment sparks initial interest and is referred to as *diversive curiosity*. This type of interest often wears off as soon as something new comes along (Leslie, 2014) or simply by the passage of time. After all, divers can only look at so many jellyfish before they want to see more. Thus, *diversive curiosity* alone will not achieve the levels of engagement and persistence necessary for deep diving. Therefore, the diving guide must use certain practices that promote persistence in learning or what is referred to as *epistemic curiosity*. When the diving guide effectively sparks epistemic curiosity, the experience progresses into a diver-lead attempt to build understanding through sustained cognitive effort (Leslie, 2014).

This scenario perfectly matches the environment in the K–5 science classroom. Even on the very best of days, we have a variety of young divers, or learners, who demonstrate a combination of diversive and epistemic curiosity from the beginning of the science learning experience. We often find a student that notices each tick of the clock and agonizes over every second. This type of student will get into the water, but he or she frequently asks, "is this for a grade?," "is this going to be on the test?," and "what do I need to do to get this right"? This learner appears to have no interest in any tasks or assignments beyond getting them completed. Yet, engagement is not a yes or no, up or down, in or out concept. Engagement falls along a spectrum. Individual levels of engagement fluctuate from day to day, class to class, and even minute to minute, requiring constant monitoring and adjusting from the boat.

Do Now

How would you describe a student who was engaged in your classroom? How would you describe a student who was not engaged in your classroom? Are all of the characteristics of engagement observable? ∎

Types of Engagement

There are three types of engagement: emotional engagement, cognitive engagement, and behavioral engagement (Fredericks, Blumenfeld, & Paris, 2004; Appleton, Christenson, & Furlong, 2008; Marks, 2000; Reschly, Huebner, Appleton, & Antaramian, 2008; Skinner, Kinderman, & Furrer, 2009). Within a given classroom, on any given day, the levels of engagement for each individual student fluctuate across these three types.

TYPE OF ENGAGEMENT	DESCRIPTION
Emotional engagement	This type of engagement relates to how the student feels both in general and about the learning.
	For example, the learner feels emotionally safe in the classroom. The learner is vested in the content, lesson, or activity. He or she has bought into what is happening in the classroom and thus feels some connection to the learning.
Cognitive engagement	This type of engagement relates to what the learner is thinking about in the classroom. This type of engagement heavily depends on the specific strategy, task, or activity developed by the teacher.
	Ideally, the learner is thinking about the content, lesson, or activity and not something outside of the classroom.
Behavioral engagement	This type of engagement refers to the actions of the student. What is the student doing? This is the most observable type of engagement.
	For example, the learner is completing the task or activity in the way it was designed by the teacher compared to a student that is off task.

Each of the three types of engagement influences the other two types of engagement, and, for a successful journey from snorkeling to scuba diving, there is a hierarchy of engagement.

Do Now

Option #1: Find a colleague, and describe the three types of engagement to him or her. Then, explain how one type influences the other two types of engagement.

Option #2: On your own and without peeking, describe the three types of engagement to yourself. Then, explain how one type influences the other two types of engagement. Look back to fill in gaps in your learning. ■

Learners that no longer feel vested in their learning because they do not buy into the specific activity or do not feel emotionally safe will likely think about something other than the science content. Subsequently, they will venture off task, behaviorally disengaging in learning. A different scenario may be that the student is *diversively curious* about the baggy of plant and animal images on his or her desk. The student then looks for some hint about the baggy, noticing a "thinking prompt" on the interactive whiteboard. "Match the parent with the offspring. Please pair the images together so that one image is the parent and one image is the offspring," 1-LS3-1 (NGSS Lead States, 2013). The student then engages in the matching activity, occasionally conversing with his or her neighbor to dialogue about the images and the task. In this scenario, the student immediately invests in the activity, which prompts him or her to think about images and how they are paired together as parent-offspring. Thus, he or she takes action and begins to physically complete the task and discuss the content with his or her peers. These scenarios represent both the relationship between the three types of engagement as well as the hierarchy of engagement: emotional, cognitive, and behavioral.

Do Now

What are some specific examples of strategies that you use to promote emotional engagement, cognitive engagement, and behavioral engagement in science learning? ∎

So, what makes an engaging strategy? In other words, from your list in the above Do-Now box, how could you self-assess the likelihood that the strategy will be an emotionally, cognitively, and behaviorally engaging strategy? In 2015, Antonetti and Garver published *17,000 Classroom Visits Can't Be Wrong*. In that book, they reported on data from, you guessed it, over 17,000 classroom walkthroughs. Embedded in the data, discovered when both Antonetti and Garver were scuba diving in their own data, were eight features of classroom tasks, activities, and strategies that were associated with sustained engagement. The following are these eight characteristics of an engaging classroom task, activity, or strategy:

1. Personal Response: Does the student have the opportunity to bring his or her own personal experiences to the learning experience? Examples

include any strategy or learning experience that invites learners to bring their own background, interests, or expertise to the conversation such as providing learners with the option to create their own analogies or metaphors, allowing learners to select how they will share their responses to a question (e.g., writing, drawing, speaking, etc.), or letting learners select the context in which a concept is explored (e.g., selection of a habitat, constellation, simple machine, or variables for an independent experiment). These examples have one thing in common: They allow learners to personalize their responses to meet their background, interests, or expertise.

2. Clear and Modeled Expectations: Does the learner have a clear understanding of what success looks like? This characteristic refers to clear learning intentions, success criteria, rubrics, and examples. Do your learners know what success looks like, or are they blindly hoping to hit the end target that you have in mind for them?

3. Sense of Audience: Does the learner have a sense that this work matters to someone other than the teacher and the grade book? Tasks that have a sense of audience are those tasks that mean something to individuals beyond the teacher. Sense of audience can be established by cooperative learning or group work where individual members have specific roles, as in a jigsaw. Other examples include community-based projects or service projects that contribute to the local, school, or classroom community (e.g., conservation projects).

4. Social Interaction: Does the learner have opportunities to socially interact with his or her peers? Although this characteristic speaks for itself, no pun intended, the value cannot be overstated. Providing learners with opportunities to talk about their learning and interact with their peers supports their meaning making and development of conceptual understanding.

5. Emotional Safety: Does the learner feel safe in asking questions or making mistakes? To be blunt, if learners feel threatened in your classroom, they will not engage. Preservation of self takes precedence over the development of wave models to explain the movement of objects.

6. Choice: Does the learner have choices in how he or she accesses the learning? As learners engage in content and process skills, we should offer choices around who they work with, what materials and manipulatives are available, and what learning strategies they can use. In addition, we should offer them multiple ways to show us what they know about the content and process in science.

7. Novelty: Does the learner experience the learning from a new or unique perspective? Learners do not pay attention to boring things. How can we present content in a way that captures their attention? Examples of this characteristic include discrepant events, demonstrations, or games and puzzles.

8. And finally, Authenticity: Does the learner experience an authentic learning experience, or is the experience sterile and unrealistic (e.g., a worksheet versus problem-solving scenario)? For example, when working with habitats, are learners engaged in a task that requires them to create an imaginary animal and the habitat in which it would survive? This is not an authentic task and will not engage learners in relevant content. Instead, we can offer them a scenario around animals on the verge of extinction and have them address the changes to their habitat that would possibly prevent them from going extinct. Authentic!

Each of the above characteristics was present in classrooms that exemplified sustained engagement but not necessarily all eight, all of the time. From their data, Antonetti and Garver (2015) reported sustained engagement 86 percent of the time when at least three characteristics were observed in a single activity, and 16 percent when only two were observed in a single activity. The percentage was approximately 0 when one or less of the characteristics were observed.

Do Now

Select several tasks, activities, and strategies that were previously presented in this book. Examine each example for the characteristics listed above. How many of the eight characteristics do they include?

Now, reflect on the tasks, activities, and strategies you implement in your classroom. How many characteristics do they include? How does this reflect the level of engagement in your science teaching and student learning? Are there adjustments you could make that would increase the levels of engagement? If so, make those adjustments. ∎

ALIGNMENT

The alignment between evidence-based strategies and the desired level of engagement facilitates the progression from snorkeler to scuba diver. Consider NGSS Standard 1-LS1-2. This particular standard aims for learners to determine patterns in behavior of parents and offspring that help offspring survive (NGSS Lead States, 2013).

1. Structure, Functions, and Information Processing
(1-LS1-2) Read texts and use media to determine patterns in behavior of parents and offspring that help offspring survive.

To accomplish this task, Mrs. Miller provided her students with three options for accessing information on patterns of behavior in parents and offspring: (1) a leveled-reader; (2) an interactive digital video; or (3) a web quest. While or after completing one of the three access options, learners were asked to complete a behaviors Venn diagram where one circle represented "parents" while the other circle represented "offspring."

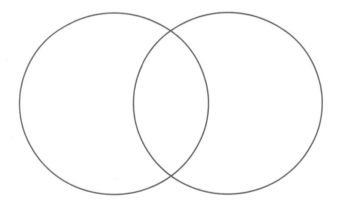

Mrs. Miller enjoyed looking at the students' diagrams and found the level of detail in each circle, as well as the overlapping area, to be reassuring that her students were scuba diving into the content by determining patterns in the behaviors: similarities and differences. From her perspective, the students emotionally, cognitively, and behaviorally engaged in the learning.

Pause and come up for air. This specific strategy, the Venn diagram, is familiar to almost every classroom teacher and certainly any reader of this book. However, we need to scuba dive into the previous scenario because there is a common, undetected problem that could lead to an unsuccessful dive. View this from the students' perspective. Your teacher has just asked you to complete a Venn diagram using one of the three options similar to Mrs. Miller's choices. What are you going to do? Really, what are you going to do? Odds are high that you will engage in one of the three options and simply put facts or excerpts from the reading, video, or web quest into one of two categories. When you notice that you have added a specific fact to both sides of the Venn diagram, you quickly erase the fact and put it in the middle. Thus, what students are really doing is identifying and sorting, not determining patterns. Mrs. Miller's assumption that her students were scuba diving into the content by determining patterns in the behaviors, similarities, and differences, is not accurate.

The Big Idea

Alignment between emotional, cognitive, and behavioral engagement and evidence-based strategies is required in the successful progression from snorkeler to scuba diver.

 ## HERE'S HOW

To address the mismatch between the strategy (a Venn diagram) and the level of engagement in the standard, Mrs. Miller next time decided to give students a Venn diagram just as in the earlier scenario. After the students filled in the information from the reading, video, or web question, she puts the learners in groups of three or four and provided them with a new graphic organizer that looked a bit different than the traditional Venn diagram (Adapted from Antonetti & Garver, 2015).

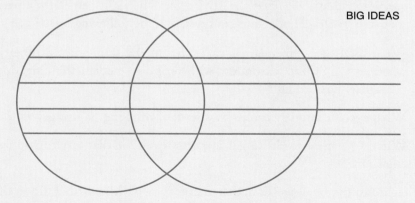

BIG IDEAS

Learners are instructed to group together differences into big ideas. Mrs. Miller provided the example of feeding. What behaviors do offspring and parents do for feeding?

(Continued)

(Continued)

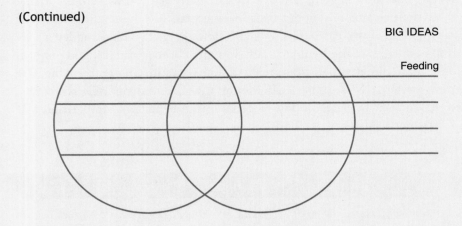

BIG IDEAS

Feeding

Learners are then given time to determine other patterns in behavior. Mrs. Miller moves through the room asking guiding questions to support learners in finding patterns associated with feeding, comforting, and protecting offspring. ■

The above Here's How points out the importance of intentionally and purposefully selecting and implementing evidence-based strategies that align with the level of engagement expected by the standard and classroom teacher. Simply drawing a strategy from your bag of tricks, even if the bag is full of evidence-based tricks, will not necessarily lead to the desired depth of engagement and learning just as floating in the water will not turn you into a boat. Similarly, a diving guide cannot simply drop individuals into the water and assume they will experience the dive just as the guide envisioned the experience. The right choice for a particular strategy or activity should take into consideration the following questions:

1. What level of engagement is called for in the standard? In other words, where in the SOLO Taxonomy, with regard to student thinking, does this particular standard fall?

2. What specific strategy evokes that level of thinking or engagement?

3. What do I need to do to get learners ready for that level of thinking or engagement?

With regard to the final question, that is exactly what Mrs. Miller did in the second scenario. Rather than throwing the Big Ideas Venn Diagram at her learners, she knew that they first needed to build and activate background knowledge. Therefore, she allowed them to make their choice for accessing the content and then allowed them to simply fill in information. Only after this part of the process did she up the level of emotional, cognitive, and behavioral engagement with the Big Ideas Venn Diagram.

Do Now

Consider the below standard, 2-LS2-1.

2. Interdependent Relationships in Ecosystems
(2LS2-1) Plan and conduct an investigation to determine if plants need sunlight and water to grow.

So now you try it. What level of thinking is required in 2-LS2-1? Where in the SOLO Taxonomy is this specific standard?

What strategies align with this same level of thinking?

Consider the following scenario: Mr. Taylor provides his students with a series of "cause" strips. He asks his students to pair up and take turns reading each "cause" strip to their partners and then their partners to describe the "effect." For example, one strip says, "Sally forgets to water her fern plant for two weeks." The partner, then, would describe the effect of Sally's forgetfulness. Students are then asked to fill in a cause-and-effect concept map, pasting the completed concept map into their interactive notebooks.

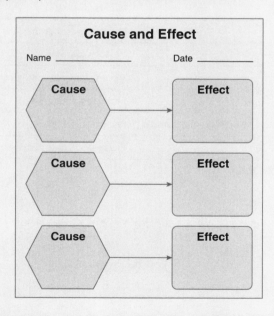

Does the level of thinking expected in this task or strategy align to the standard? Why, or why not?

Are there changes you could make for better alignment between emotional, cognitive, and behavioral engagement and evidence-based strategies? ∎

EVIDENCE-BASED STRATEGIES

In 2009, Professor John Hattie published the book *Visible Learning: A Synthesis of Over 800 Meta–Analyses Relating to Achievement* (2009). A collection of over 1,200 meta-analyses involving a quarter of a billion students from across the world, the *Visible Learning* research provides the most comprehensive collection of research that not only answers the question what works but also the question what works best. Put differently, there are strategies that are not associated with student achievement, strategies that are minimally associated with student achievement, and then strategies that are associated with gains above and beyond 1 year worth of growth. That's right, there are *high–yield strategies* that show greater gains than are expected in a typical school year. Therefore, the repository of high-yield, evidence-based practices is the *Visible Learning* research (Hattie, 2009, 2012).

Table of Evidence-Based Practices

HIGH-YIELD, EVIDENCE-BASED STRATEGIES AND/OR PRACTICES	
Cognitive task analysis (breaking down the task)	Classroom discussion
Effective feedback	Formative assessment or checks for understanding
Concept mapping	Vocabulary programs
Distributed practice	Mastery learning
Cooperative learning	Meta-cognitive strategies
Questioning	Small group learning
Interventions for learners with special needs	Reciprocal teaching
Self-questioning	Engagement and teacher clarity

SOURCE: (Hattie, 2009, 2012)

Do Now

Select three or four of the items from the table of high-yield, evidence-based strategies. How would you implement or use these strategies so that they also include the eight characteristics or features of an engaging learning experience? ∎

	STRATEGY #1	STRATEGY #2	STRATEGY #3	STRATEGY #4
Personal response				
Clear and modeled expectations				
Sense of audience				
Social interaction				
Emotional safety				
Choice				
Novelty				
Authenticity				

There are approximately 200 strategies and practices (see www.visible-learning .org) in the *Visible Learning* database. Again, not all of the 200 strategies and practices are high-yield strategies or practices. The 16 presented in the previous chart are all high-yield and are associated with more than 1 year worth of growth in student achievement.

Do Now

Review and select five strategies and practices from the previous chart of high-yield, evidence-based strategies to use as you complete the Do-Now exercise. Use the thinking organizer below to record your thoughts and ideas. ■

HIGH-YIELD EVIDENCE-BASED STRATEGIES AND/OR PRACTICES	EXAMPLES MODELED OR PRESENTED IN THIS BOOK	HOW YOU USE THE STRATEGY/PRACTICE, OR HOW YOU WILL USE THE STRATEGY/PRACTICE?

One evidence-based practice is the use of science content as a context for the development of fluency and comprehension skills. With this in mind, let's examine a few literacy examples. We will target the three phases of reading: prereading, during reading, and after reading.

Prereading. Strategies for prereading are designed to get students thinking about the content, make predictions (e.g., self-questioning), and activate prior knowledge. These activities can be done individually or through cooperative learning and small groups. The goal of these activities is to give students a framework into which they will fit the content obtained from reading (e.g., engagement and teacher clarity).

HERE'S HOW

Prereading Strategies

1. Have students quickly peruse the reading selection and write down a brief summary or prediction of what they will learn from the reading in their interactive notebooks.

2. In a cooperative learning, small group, or whole group setting, brainstorm what they already know about the topic presented in the reading selection. A Know-Want-Learn (KWL) works well for this particular brainstorming session.

3. Make a list of key vocabulary terms that will be presented in the reading. Have students describe the words or predict what they think the words mean.

4. Develop a list of questions about the content.

5. Look at the visuals or graphics contained within the section or chapter. Discuss and share any interesting visuals or graphics you discovered with a neighbor or the class. Have students respond to the following question: Why do you think the authors included this particular visual or graphic? ▪

Do Now

Continue on with the list. What other strategies could you implement in your classroom? ▪

Notice that the prereading activities are also high-yield, evidence-based strategies that strive to engage learners at all three levels: emotional, cognitive, and behavioral. Simply put, these strategies are effective when initially guiding students into the diving environment. When using these prereading strategies, it is important to have students write down their thinking in either their interactive notebooks or on poster paper so that it is visible to you and the learners and so the thinking can be revisited during and after reading. Finally, these strategies work for digital text and other multimedia environments.

During Reading. While students engage in content, it is absolutely vital for students to break the learning into segments so that practice is distributed over a longer period of time. Specifically, for reading, after each segment, students should stop and think about the reading to self-check their understanding or engage in an explicit activity so that the teacher can check their understanding.

 HERE'S HOW

During Reading Strategies

1. Have students complete fill-in notes as they read. This is often called a reading guide.

2. Have students stop after certain segments and write a summary about the information they just read.

3. Students might develop or complete a graphic organizer for each segment of the reading.

4. After reading a particular segment in class, have students turn to a neighbor and discuss the content. Share "ah-ha" moments, surprises, or questions they may have.

5. As students come across answers to the prereading questions or vocabulary terms, edit and revise the prereading information to make sure it is accurate.

6. Engage your students in a focused reading.

    While reading

    put an (*) next to something you want to remember,

    an (!) when the information is an essential piece of information,

    a (check mark) when the information agrees with your thinking, and

    a (?) when the information has raised a question.

    These notations will also assist with follow-up discussions. ∎

Do Now

Continue on with the list. What other strategies could you implement in your classroom? ■

After Reading. After the reading is complete, students need to continue to process the information. Beyond completing a packet or worksheet at the end of the section or chapter, students should have multiple opportunities to make meaning of the content.

HERE'S HOW

After Reading Strategies

1. Develop an elevator speech about the major ideas, concepts, or topics from the reading.

2. Create a brochure or book cover that presents the information from the reading.

3. Develop a reading quiz and answer key to exchange with another student.

4. Create graphic organizer for the reading.

5. Using the Cornell Notes template, create a set of notes for the reading.

6. Develop a game (e.g., Jeopardy, Taboo, $100,000 Pyramid, Who Wants to Be a Millionaire?, etc.) for the key vocabulary from the reading. ■

Do Now

Continue on with the list. What other strategies could you implement in your classroom? ■

You can increase the level of engagement by making conscious decisions to embed different types of strategies or use them simultaneously. The goal for any strategy is to make student thinking visible to the teacher and to the learner. This, in the end, is the big idea behind the *Visible Learning* research (Hattie, 2009). Anytime learners' behavior can be observed, monitored, or measured, they are exhibiting an overt response (Corno, 1993; Pintrich, 2004; Schunk & Zimmerman, 2003; Vrugt & Oort, 2008; Finn, 1989, 1993; Finn & Voelkl, 1993). Teachers successfully engage their students in many overt strategies throughout any given day. Some of these observable behaviors are creating a nonlinguistic representation, engaging in a peer conversation, drafting an advance organizer, or performing a demonstration. All of these methods can be observed, measured, or monitored by both the teacher and learners. To ensure that learners are progressing from snorkeler to scuba diver, overt engagement must make thinking visible in a way that provides a clear representation of that thinking. Simply asking learners, "does everyone understand?" is risky because some learners, if not many of your students, will simply nod their heads yes to avoid standing out. Thus, overt strategies should do the following:

1. Align with the level of thinking associated with the standard and the specific task, activity, or strategy—For example, if the content standard asks students to compare and contrast, does your question, task, or assignment ask them to engage at that same level or does it ask them to simply name or identify (Almarode & Miller, 2013)?

2. Require students to discuss and explain concepts to their peers—No single strategy provides a better opportunity to deeply engage in content than having to teach content to another person so that he or she understands it (Medina, 2014b).

3. Ask students to reason with evidence—Do you ask students to support their responses by explicitly asking, "what makes you say that?"

4. Offer multiple opportunities for students to make explicit connections— Using writing prompts, discussion circles, or graphic organizers, have students explicitly unpack how "this" relates to "that."

5. Never tell the students the whole story—Instead, provide them with opportunities to explore the data and, on their own, extract the big ideas and form conclusions. Of course, once they identify the big idea or form a conclusion, always ask "what makes you say that?"

6. Ensure that instructional experiences provide multiple exposures, through different lenses, and from different perspectives (Ritchhart, Church, & Morrison, 2011).

Then there are the behaviors that cannot be seen, measured, or monitored. Anytime you ask your students to think, imagine, visualize, or go over something in their minds, you are asking them to perform a covert behavior (Appleton, Christenson, Kim, & Reschly, 2006; Corno, 1993; Pintrich, 2004; Schunk & Zimmerman, 2003; Vrugt & Oort, 2008; Finn, 1989, 1993; Finn & Voelkl, 1993). Even though you cannot observe, hear, measure, or monitor the task given, if the students are performing the requested task, it is active engagement. Thus, providing students with a covert task (e.g., self-questioning or metacognition) maximizes the opportunities for emotional, cognitive, and behavioral engagement.

Much of the thinking done in formal education has been aimed at skills of analysis. As students engage themselves in many of the 21st-century learning skills, they will be exhibiting covert thinking skills. This includes teaching learners how to mentally estimate answers, identify and eliminate irrelevant information, and critically think about the logical solutions. When we request these tasks, we are creating covert learning experiences for our students. As they prepare to go out in the working world, the corporate world is telling us that the focus is much more on exploring ideas, generating possibilities, and looking for multiple answers than ever before. Developing the thinking skills of your students is becoming a vital part of education. This is only one reason why it is essential for teachers to make conscious decisions to embed both overt and covert levels of engagement. After all, you hope your scuba divers covertly engage in the diving environment so that you can stay on the boat.

When used separately, the student(s) you intentionally involve in an overt strategy (e.g., putting a something on the board, explaining a particular concept, or answering a question) are highly engaged; however, too often this limits the opportunities for many students in the class to engage. Teachers are often occupied with the students who are requested to be engaged and don't even realize that a large percentage of the students are waiting or tuning out. Put yourself in their shoes. If a teacher calls on a student to describe the difference between living and nonliving factors in an ecosystem, in most cases, the other classmates are either relieved because they were not called on or disappointed that they were not allowed to show off their knowledge of ecosystems. In both cases, the odds of them checking out for this period of time are probably quite high. So, the next time you ask a student or several students to go up to the interactive whiteboard to fill in the lifecycle of a butterfly, simultaneously assign a covert thinking activity to the other students in the room. This is a great opportunity to stimulate higher level thinking, embed creative thought, or develop problem-solving skills in all learners. Reflective questioning that evokes reflecting thinking in divers as they engage in the diving environment increases the likelihood that they will transfer this experience to a new and different context, which is exactly where we are headed in the next chapter.

EXIT TICKET

Revisit the success criteria associated with this chapter.

1. I can compare and contrast the different types of engagement in the science classroom.

2. I can explain the relationship between student engagement and the selection of teaching and learning strategies.

3. I can match specific teaching and learning strategies with the level of engagement I expect in learners.

Using the following Likert scales, reflect on and evaluate your own learning:

I can compare and contrast the different types of engagement in the science classroom.

○————————————————○————————————————○

Got It   **Getting There**   **Not Yet**

Evidence:

I can explain the relationship between student engagement and the selection of teaching and learning strategies.

○————————————————○————————————————○

Got It   **Getting There**   **Not Yet**

Evidence:

I can match specific teaching and learning strategies with the level of engagement I expect in learners.

Got It — Getting There — Not Yet

Evidence:

List at least three ideas or concepts you want to remember from this chapter.

Describe at least two strategies you will take away from this chapter and try out in your classroom.

What is one challenge you will face as you implement the ideas from this chapter?

CHAPTER 7

From Snorkelers to Scuba Divers

Preparing for the Next Dive, Step #3—Focus on Learning, Not Just Performance

Learning Intention

I understand that there is a difference between performance and learning in my science classroom and that this influences transfer of learning.

Success Criteria

By the end of this chapter, the following success criteria will be met:

1. I can differentiate between learner performance and learning in the science classroom.

2. I can identify three cognitive principles that promote transfer and long-term learning.

3. I can explain the role of desirable difficulties in learning science.

Up to this point in our journey, we have worked through the metaphor of the journey to deep learning by creating comparisons to snorkeling and scuba diving. References to getting learners in the water, ensuring learners have the necessary equipment and preparation for the dive, selecting the ideal diving environment, and supporting learners as they navigate the diving environment. Each of these references is adjusted based on the learners' prior and background knowledge, the nature of their thinking, and the nature of their interaction with the learning environment.

Do Now

In the following table, and without looking back through the previous chapters, take a moment and think back on the main ideas, topics, concepts, and examples from those previous chapters. How can the metaphor of a snorkeler and scuba diver be applied to learners' prior and background knowledge, nature of thinking, and the nature of interactions? Finally, in the last column, what does this look like in the classroom? If you cannot retrieve the information at this time or feel as if your information is incomplete, fill in what you can and then look back once you have attempted to fill in each spot in the table. ■

	METAPHOR	TRANSFER TO CLASSROOM ENVIRONMENT
Prior and background knowledge		
Nature of thinking		
Nature of interactions		

So, what happens next? In the classroom, the ultimate goal for a teacher is that his or her students will transfer their learning to similar contexts and even contexts that, at first glance, appear to be very different from the original learning environment. For example, in 1-LS3-1, a student that knows and understands that young plants and animals do not always look like their parents will hopefully transfer that understanding to subsequent learning about inheritance, metamorphosis, and hybrids.

1. Structure, Function, and Information Processing
(1-LS3-1) Make observations to construct an evidence-based account that young plants and animals are like, but not exactly like, their parents.

In addition, the first-grade teacher hopes that the learner will make deep connections to patterns in the growth and development of organisms to patterns of change in other contexts like weather, geologic time, cultures, mathematical models, and even the writing process (e.g., prewriting, rough drafting, editing, and revising). For snorkelers and scuba divers, this is also the goal of the person in the boat. After completing a dive, the guide in the boat hopes that the experiences from the initial dive will transfer to subsequent dives, enhancing the overall journey of each diver.

When learners transfer learning from one context to a similar, although not identical, context it is referred to as near transfer (Bransford, Brown, & Cocking, 2000; Hattie, Fisher, & Frey, 2017; Perkins & Salomon, 1992). When original context appears quite dissimilar to another context (e.g., the life cycle of a butterfly and the writing process), this is called far transfer. Far transfer requires learners to engage in a deliberate and effortful search for connections.

 ## HERE'S HOW

Ms. Frost expects her young learners to understand the big idea or theme of *change* across the content areas. She recognizes that to promote far transfer, she must engage her scuba divers in learning experiences that require them to deliberately find connections beyond surface-level characteristics. Ms. Frost puts four topics on the whiteboard:

Animal Life Cycles

Ancient Civilizations

Mathematical Patterns

The Writing Process

Learners are placed in preselected pairs, provided poster paper and markers, and asked to find the common theme underlying each of these topics. She tells them, "Please be prepared to reason with evidence when you share your ideas." ∎

PERFORMANCE VERSUS LEARNING

The Big Idea
Teaching for transfer, regardless of whether the learning intention is for near or far transfer, requires intentional and purposeful learning experiences and a focus on just that, learning, and not simply performance.

Performance refers to how successfully the learner can recall or retrieve information immediately after the educational experience. *Learning* refers to how well the learning has been encoded by the learner for recall, retrieval, and transfer in the future (Yan, Clark, & Bjork, 2017). "Without a deliberate awareness of and attention to the distinction between learning and performance, it is easy for both [teachers] and learners to fall prey to illusions of learning" (Yan et al., 2017, p. 72). Classroom teachers that focus on performance, even though they may not be aware that they are focused solely on performance, assess student learning by only the current performance of their learners rather than reassessing learning multiple times and later on in the day, week, month, semester, and year. Similarly, learners self-assess and draw false conclusions about their learning based on their performance or current score on an assignment prepared at the last minute through, say, cramming. For snorkelers and scuba divers, this would be the belief that you have mastered the skill of scuba diving simply because today's dive went very well. As mentioned in Chapter 2, Richard Mayer (2011) defines learning as "change in knowledge attributable to experience (p. 14)." Incorporating the difference between learning and performance, we can now say, learning is a change in what the learner understands, knows, and is able to do as a result of some experience that is both durable and flexible in the future.

Do Now

Think about the teaching and learning in your classroom. Do you focus on performance or learning? Provide specific examples as evidence to support your answer. ■

The previous discussion, as well as the above Do-Now brings the illusions of learning to the surface. There are several that, if not addressed, will be barriers to preparing divers for the next dive.

Do Now

Here are several statements about learning. Please indicate whether you believe the statement is true, supported by research, or false, refuted by research. ▪

	YOUR ANSWER	ANSWER SUPPORTED BY RESEARCH
1. Learners remember everything. They sometimes cannot retrieve science learning at certain times.		
2. Offering learners the opportunity to struggle with science ideas or concepts leads to better learning.		
3. Rote rehearsal and repetition of basic facts leads to better learning.		
4. Praising effort, instead of achievement, leads to better learning outcomes.		

As we move through the next few sections of this chapter, we present research that either supports or refutes the previous statements. For now, let's just say that the only statement from the above table that is true is Statement 2. In fact, the reason that Statements 1, 3, and 4 are false is because Statement 2 is true. Statement 2 is what researchers refer to as a desirable difficulty or a strategy that emotionally, cognitively, and behaviorally engages a learner in effortful and elaborative learning (Bjork & Bjork, 2014). The effortful and elaborate aspect of these strategies is what earns them the title of difficulties. Yet, these difficulties lead to the desired outcomes of long-term learning and not simply performance. In other words, strategies or tasks that make the learning appear to be fast and easy will not support learners' ability to recall or retrieve the information in the future (Yan et al., 2017). Learners need to engage in desirable difficulties to promote transfer and prepare for the next dive.

Do Now

Talk to your learners. What strategies or tasks do your students believe work best in their learning? Why? Using the list generated from talking to your students, which of those strategies or tasks would be considered desirable difficulties? Which of those strategies or tasks make learning appear too fast and easy? ▪

What makes desirable difficulties difficult for teachers to implement and students to engage in is that they initially appear ineffective and inefficient (Yan et al., 2017). In fact, desirable difficulties often cause a drop in short-term performance that is disconcerting for both the teacher and the learner. Thus, they abandon these strategies for those that make it appear that students are more quickly learning the content. However, this is performance focused and not learning focused. A healthy struggle now pays off later. As learners continue in their journey from snorkeler to scuba diver we must create desirable difficulties, along with the patience to persist through the initial drop in performance. In the end, desirable difficulties are the most robust techniques for long-term learning (Bjork, 1994). Three desirable difficulties will support this learning journey by ensuring that your young learners acquire high quality information, engage in evidence-based practices or strategies, and practice applying their learning to new contexts:

Elaborate Encoding

Retrieval Practice

The Spacing Effect

ELABORATE ENCODING

Elaborate encoding involves learners processing the science content in a way that allows them to make meaning of the information (Craik, 2002; Craik & Lockhart, 1972; Craik & Tulving, 1975). Consider the following scenario in Mr. Wiley's first-grade classroom.

Mr. Wiley is introducing the idea that the amount of daylight changes at different times of the year. His learning goal is for students to make relative comparisons between the four seasons and the amount of daylight.

1. Space Systems: Patterns and Cycles
(1-ESS1-2) Make observations at different times of year to relate the amount of daylight to the time of year.

Which of the following options represent an approach that uses the desirable difficulty of elaborate encoding?

Option #1:

Mr. Wiley shows a brief Brain Pop video on the position of the Earth relative to the Sun and then asks his students to complete a handout on the four seasons and the amount of daylight. He asks his learners to use this sheet to prepare for the upcoming assessment.

Option #2:

Mr. Wiley presents data on the amount of daylight and the time of year to his students.

FIGURE 7.1

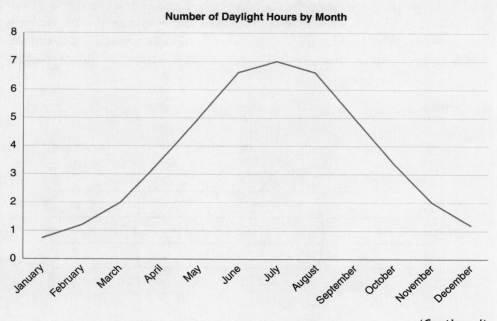

Number of Daylight Hours by Month

(Continued)

After providing an overview of the x and y axes, Mr. Wiley asks his students to work with their shoulder partners to develop a list of conclusions that they can generate from the graph as well as a list of questions they have about the information.

Option #2 represents elaborate encoding because the strategy associated with the content requires learners to process the science content in a way that allows them to make meaning of the information. Although the learners may initially struggle with the content, this desirable difficulty will enhance learning and develop meta-cognitive skills for life-long scuba diving.

Renowned author of the book *Brain Rules*, John Medina (2014b) identified three necessary components of meaning making. First, learners must have opportunities to visualize the information. In this context, visualizing refers to the ability of the learner to form an internal mental representation of the content. For example, in 4-PS3-3 learners are expected to predict outcomes about the changes in energy that occur when objects collide (NGSS Lead States, 2013).

4. Energy
(4-PS3-3) Ask questions and predict outcomes about the changes in energy that occur when objects collide.

Providing multiple concrete, authentic demonstrations allows each individual learner to mentally represent the concepts beyond the abstract textbook definitions. Second, learners must have opportunities to find patterns across multiple examples. Referring back to 4-PS3-3, learners should identify similarities and differences between various physical scenarios that involve colliding objects.

FIGURE 7.2

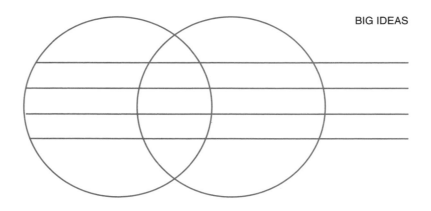

BIG IDEAS

The enhanced Venn diagram (adapted from Antonetti & Garver, 2015) from Chapter 6 could provide the thinking structure for such a task. Finally, learners must be able to incorporate their own emotion into the content.

Do Now

Does this really work? Does elaborate encoding enhance learning? A psychologist by the name of Pusateri (2003) tested this very hypothesis. Let's replicate a variation of the experiment. Gather a group of friends, colleagues, or use your own students. Divide them into two groups. Let them know that you will be showing them a list of 20 words. Before showing them the list of words, give instructions to both groups.

The first group should keep count in their mind the number of words that contain the letter E. That's it; have them count the number of words containing the letter E. The second group should look at each word and decide if the word makes them think of pleasant thoughts or not so pleasant thoughts. Neither group should write anything down at this point. Show them the list of words, and give them 2 minutes.

After 2 minutes, hide the list and have them write down as many words as they can remember from the list of 20.

Which group members recalled the most words? Why do you think so? ■

Elaborate encoding is a desirable difficulty that enhances learning through scuba diving. This type of deep processing allows learners to make meaning of the content and thus create stronger representation of the information, recognizing patterns, and invoking emotion (Medina, 2014b). What is worth noting here is that there are patterns in what characterizes elaborate encoding and Marzano's elements of direct vocabulary instruction. If you recall from Chapter 4, direct vocabulary instruction should require students to (1) develop descriptions of words rather than just definitions; (2) incorporate both linguistic and nonlinguistic representations; (3) include multiple exposures to the words or concepts; (4) encourage students to discuss the words or concepts; (5) require students to play with words; and (6) focus on words that are necessary for academic success (Marzano, 2004; Marzano & Pickering, 2005). Simply put, academic vocabulary must be elaborately encoded so that learners can put the vocabulary to good use. The same goes for all science content.

Just like Mr. Wiley, we have choices about how learners encode content knowledge and process skills. The following examples provide meaning-making opportunities for learners. That is, learners have opportunities to look at the information through their multiple ways of representing the content (e.g., graphically, verbally, with questions, etc.). Second, learners have opportunities to find patterns between these representations and their own experiences in life. Finally, learners are able to emotionally invest in their learning. Social interaction, choice, personal response, novelty, and authenticity evoke this vested interest in the content.

HERE'S HOW

The think-tac-toe board is one strategy that facilitates elaborate encoding. Learners have choices about which tasks they will complete to get "think-tac-toe." Choice provides the emotional connection while the purposefully and intentionally designed tasks provide the other two components of meaning making: visualizing and patterns. ∎

4. Energy
(4-ESS3-1) Obtain and combine information to describe that energy and fuels are derived from natural resources and their uses affect the environment.

Pollution

Select one product that pollutes. Develop a skit that explains the effects this product has on the environment. Be prepared to act out this skit with a classmate.	Illustrate or take pictures of several things that cause pollution. Label your illustrations or pictures, and write a paragraph about how each item causes or contributes to pollution.	What is the leading cause of pollution in our world today? With a classmate, be prepared to debate this question in front of the class.
You are concerned about the different habitats that are struggling with high levels of pollution. Develop and illustrate a pamphlet that will inform others about this situation.	Pollution does not happen overnight. Design a series of cartoon strips showing the progression of pollution over a number of years. Show some of the causes for the increase in the amount of pollution.	You have a product that will reduce pollution. Create a poster that will promote the use of your product. Be prepared to share a slogan for your product with the class.

(Continued)

(Continued)

Spend some time collecting items that cause pollution. Write a paragraph about each item explaining why you collected that item and how it contributes to the pollution in our environment.	Take a walk for the purpose of collecting information about the nonrecyclable materials you find around (inside and outside) our school. Create a report based on your findings, and be prepared to share your information with the class.	Select a particular polluted habitat. Create a newsletter informing others about this area, and give ideas about how to improve or help this situation.

 HERE'S HOW

Project-based learning tasks provide elaborate encoding opportunities as well. When supported by teacher questioning and feedback, these tasks provide authentic experiences with science content. ■

FIGURE 7.3

Science
Design Brief   **Music Makers**

Background: We know that sound is a form of energy produced and transmitted by vibrating matter and that pitch is determined by the frequency of a vibrating object. You have been studying sound and how sound is transmitted and used as a means of communication.

Design challenge: Design and build a musical instrument that will make at least three different pitches, and use it to create a tune of your own. You must use the materials that your teacher provides.

Criteria:
Your instrument must
- have at least three different recognizable pitches
- be accompanied by a paragraph explaining how your instrument works
- use only the materials provided by your teacher
- be attractive and neatly made
- be used to play a short tune

Materials: You may select from the items below.
- straws
- card stock
- rubber bands
- craft sticks
- 6 inches of tape
- paper clips
- paper cups
- balloons
- tissue paper
- 24 inches of string

RETRIEVAL PRACTICE

Once a learner has elaborately encoded information from a think-tac-toe board or a project-based learning task, continued scuba diving also depends on retrieval practice. This is memory maintenance. Retrieval practice refers to the act of retrieving information from previous learning experiences. That is, can your learners retrieve the water cycle from their memory systems? As a word of caution, retrieval practice is not just repetition. Try this next experiment.

Do Now

Of the 15 pennies in the picture below, which one is the correct image of a penny? Only one is the correct image. ∎

FIGURE 7.4

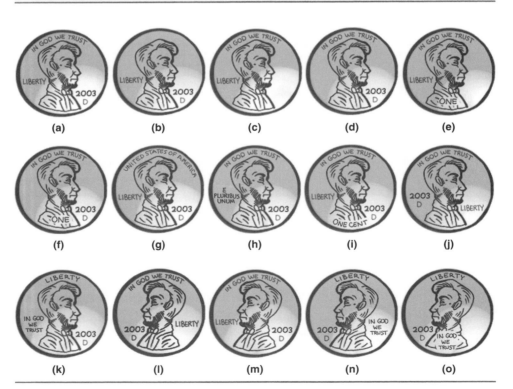

SOURCE: Adapted from Stangor, C. (2012). Remembering and judging. In *Beginning psychology V 1.0* (pp. 399-400). Retrieved from https://2012books.lardbucket.org/books/beginnning-psychology/index .html

How difficult was the previous Do-Now? You more than likely had to locate a real penny to verify your answer (which is *a*). However, we have all seen hundreds if not thousands of pennies in our lifetime: repetition. So clearly repetition alone is not the answer to retrieval practice, otherwise you would be able to draw a perfect penny from memory. Completing an assignment of a "gazillion" science questions in a packet or reviewing a mile-high stack of flashcards is not going to enhance learning or the desire to scuba dive in the future. Retrieval practice is a desirable difficulty. The harder a learner has to work to retrieve the information, the stronger the memory becomes. One strategy that promotes retrieval practice is fill-in notes. Take a look at the following statements about retrieval practice, and see if you can fill in the blanks.

Do Now

1. Instead of repeated restu_____, learners are far better off tes_____ themselves, both early and often (Roediger & Karpicke, 2006).

2. This does not mean that we admi_____ more tests but rather provide numerous

   opp_____ for students to actively retr_____ previously learned information from memory (Roediger & Karpicke, 2006).

3. The act of retr_____ is a memory modi_____. Whatever infor_____ is retr_____ becomes strengthened (Bjork, 1994). ∎

ANSWERS

Instead of repeated RESTUDYING, learners are far better off TESTING themselves, both early and often (Roediger & Karpicke, 2006). This does not mean that we ADMINISTER more tests but rather provide numerous OPPORTUNITIES for students to actively RETRIEVE previously learned information from memory (Roediger & Karpicke, 2006). The act of RETRIEVAL is a memory MODIFIER. Whatever INFORMATION is RETRIEVED becomes strengthened (Bjork, 1994).

Let's look at two specific strategies that provide numerous opportunities for students to actively retrieve previously learned information through this desirable difficulty.

HERE'S HOW

The strategy, blackout, is a cooperative learning strategy. Students are placed in partners or groups of no larger than five students. Each group is provided a pad of sticky notes and a blackout board for the particular standard, content, or topic. We provide two examples related to weather. Example #1 is for younger learners, while Example #2 is for upper elementary students. Once the group decides who should go first, that learner selects a square and provides a response to the question or task. The other members of the group provide follow-up questioning or feedback to this first student. Once everyone is satisfied that the particular square has been thoroughly addressed, the learners place a sticky note on that square to black it out. The board is passed to the next student, and the process is repeated. This continues until the teacher decides to end the retrieval practice or the group's board is completely blacked out.

3. Weather and Climate	
(3-ESS2-1) Represent data in tables and graphic displays to describe typical weather conditions expected during a particular season.	

Weather Example #1

Rain	Clouds
Snow	Sunlight
Wind	Temperature

Rain:

Compare rain to snow. How it is the same? How is it different?

Clouds:

Look at our weather chart, did we have more cloudy days or sunny days this month?

Snow:

What are some of the things you can do with snow?

Sunlight:

What does sunlight do to the temperature and the weather?

Wind:

What does wind make you think of? What comes to your mind when you think of wind?

Temperature:

What tools or instruments do we use to measure temperature?

Weather Example #2 ■

When describing the difference between weather and climate I get confused about _____?	Share with your group how wind direction and speed is determined, labeled, and communicated.	Share with the group your thoughts about how wind and temperature are related. For example, does water freeze faster when the wind is blowing?
Start a conversation about the differences between sleet and hail. Use their individual characteristics to describe those differences.	Based on the data on the other side of this paper, what season of the year would you predict is occurring, and why?	If I analyze the climate currently happening here in our state, I would assume that _____ (where in the world) would be experiencing a climate similar to ours?
Offer the group some suggestions on how to prevent or reduce the amount of flowing within a flood zone.	During the winter, I would expect to experience _____. (what forms of weather hazards)	Share with your group some of the ways scientists would describe, predict, or prevent an avalanche?

 HERE'S HOW

Wage a Bet

Divide your class up into small groups, about 4 students per group.

- Provide each team a 3 × 3 table already printed or have them drawn one on a sheet of paper.

(Continued)

(Continued)

- Select nine essential concepts, terms, or learnings associated with the unit the class is currently working on or has recently completed.

- After posting these terms either on poster paper, a whiteboard, or smart board, have the students randomly write one term in each box.

- Tell the groups to assign each term a value, based on the confidence level of their collective knowledge of that content.

  100-150-200-250-300-350-400-450-500

- The goal is to obtain the highest amount of points. The teacher either gives a problem or asks a question in each area. After each question, the group members put their heads together to come up with an answer or solution.

- If the group gets the response correct, the members circle the point value. If the group does not get it right, they cross out the point value. After all nine questions are asked, they add up their total point value.

Here is a specific example.

5. Structure and Properties of Matter
(5-PS1-1) Develop a model to describe that matter is made of particles too small to be seen.
(5-PS1-2) Measure and graph quantities to provide evidence that regardless of the type of change that occurs when heating, cooling, or mixing substances, the total weight of matter is conserved.
(5-PS1-3) Make observations and measurements to identify materials based on their properties.
(5-PS1-4) Conduct an investigation to determine whether the mixing of two or more substances results in new substances.

Directions: As a team, write one term in each box. (Location does not matter)

➢ Mass

➢ Matter

➢ Mixture

➢ Gases

➢ Compound

➢ Molecule

➢ Physical Change

➢ Element

➢ Liquids

- Assign a value to each term. Write that value in the corresponding box.

100-150-200-250-300-350-400-450-500

- The point values are based on how confident your group is on answering a question correctly based on that term.

So, a group's box could look like this:

Element 300	Mass 500	Compound 100
Liquids 350	Molecule 200	Gases 250
Physical Change 50	Mixture 150	Matter 450

- One at a time, ask the following questions:

- The questions can be orally communicated, projected on slides, or written on your smart board.

- Students should be given time to discuss and record their group response.

Mass

Question:

Explain the difference between mass and weight?

Answer:

Mass is the amount of matter in an object, and weight is the gravitational pull on the object.

Matter

Question:

What causes matter to change states?

Answer:

Temperature determines the state of a substance.

(*Continued*)

(Continued)

Mixture

Question:

How is a mixture different from a solution?

Answer:

A mixture is a combination of two or more substances that do not lose their identifying characteristics when combined. A solution is a mixture in which one substance dissolves in another.

Gases

Question:

A change directly from the solid to the gaseous state without becoming liquid is called _____?

Answer:

Sublimation

Compound

Question:

How is a compound formed? Explain why water is a compound.

Answer:

When two or more elements combine to form a new substance, it is called a compound. Examples include water (H2O) and table salt (NaCl).

Molecule

Question:

What is the difference between a compound and a molecule?

Answer:

A molecule is formed when two or more atoms join together chemically. A compound is a molecule that contains at least two different elements. All compounds are molecules, but not all molecules are compounds.

Physical Change

Question:

How is a chemical change different than a physical change?

Answer:

During a chemical change, the chemical identity of the substance is changed. During a physical change, the chemical identity remains the same, but the state of matter or physical property changes.

Element

Question:

Provide an example of an element, and then explain why it is an element.

Answer:

An element is a substance made up of just one type of atom. Gold is an element made up of just one type of atom.

Liquids

Question:

What do we call the process of changing from a gas into a liquid?

Answer:

Condensation

- After each question, give students enough time to come up with their answers.

- Engage the students in a discussion that extends their thought process. We want this to be a productive collaborative session so that other students understand the rationale for each answer. ■

THE SPACING EFFECT

Elaborately encoded: check. Retrieval practice beyond simple repetition: check. One remaining question, especially in the age of accountability, standards, and standardized test, is the frequency of such retrieval. How often do my learners need to engage in retrieval practice so that I see significant gains in learning? The answer is simple: Learners should engage in retrieval practice as soon as they have started to forget.

Do Now

Following is the Ebbinghaus Forgetting Curve (Cepeda, Pashler, Vul, Wixted, & Rohrer, 2006). Take a few minutes to study the graph. Once you have had some time to study and reflect on the graph, please complete the following columned chart. ■

(Continued)

(Continued)

FIGURE 7.5

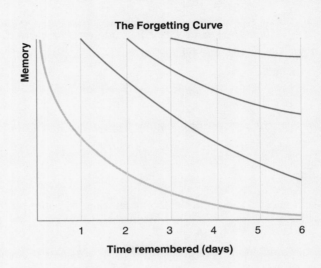

The Forgetting Curve

Memory

Time remembered (days)

What inferences can you draw from the graph? List at least five inferences	What questions do you have about the graph? Provide at least three questions	How is this data helpful to your teaching and students' learning?

The Ebbinhaus data support the idea that overtime we will forget. Snorkeling or successfully scuba diving today does not guarantee that our learners can pull off a repeat dive next week. Even with the other desirable difficulties in place, elaborate encoding and retrieval practice, ensuring that we space out retrieval practice so that it, too, becomes a desirable difficulty is critical to long-term learning outcomes as well as future dives. However, it is not realistic for any teacher to know the exact moment when each of his or her students is forgetting. Thus, we have to constantly monitor and provide multiple opportunities for retrieval practice throughout the day, week, month, and year.

Retrieval practice through formative assessment is a systematic approach used to monitor and adjust daily instruction based on learners' thinking. An essential component of academic success involves both the teacher and the student actively and continuously monitoring student learning through specific strategies designed to gather information on student learning. As the guide in the boat, checks for understanding are designed and implemented to decrease forgetting, to fill in gaps, and to encourage students to think about ideas, concepts, or topics in a way that makes learning a long-lasting experience. Spacing them out ensures that you have waited just long enough for learners to begin to forget.

These strategies have been modeled throughout the entire book. It is all about keeping the end in mind. What is your desired outcome, performance, or learning? If you selected learning, then we must create an environment that creates desirable difficulties for each student.

As a teacher gathers information to make instructional decisions, it is essential that this information be visible, monitored, and measured. Retrieval practice through formative assessment is most effective when the teacher uses strategies that elicit an observable form of student thinking. The student must develop and then share his or her thinking in an overt manner that aligns directly to learning objectives. The process of developing and sharing a response in a clear and effective manner requires retrieval and then feedback. The response must be checked. Teachers must examine and analyze student responses in order to identify what has been learned, see possible gaps in the student's knowledge, and gather insight that will be used to provide the student with meaningful feedback. If these components are done effectively, not only will teachers improve their ability to monitor and adjust their instruction, but they will be putting structures into place that actually hold students accountable for thinking about their learning. Retrieval should be a routine, not an occasional, occurrence.

As the story goes, a future teacher was sitting in a college education course many years ago when the professor stood up and told a story about his two children. They were in his backyard on a beautiful summer afternoon attempting to catch butterflies. As with any story, students sitting in the class can often make a personal connection to the story. For example, you may have immediately thought of

catching lightning bugs, which was a favorite childhood experience. The professor continued to explain that, in a short period of time, his son had caught over a half a dozen butterflies. Just about the time the professor and his two sons were going to stop, he heard his son crying. When the concerned professor looked toward his son, he noticed that his son had left off the top of the container, and all the butterflies had flown away.

The professor paused for a moment and then said to the classroom full of future teachers, I want you to close your eyes and picture my son sitting there and all the butterflies flying away over his head. He continued to point out that every time you decide not to engage your students in a closure activity at the end of your lesson, that is exactly what will happen to all the knowledge you tried to put into your students' brains. When closure is implemented correctly, it is a retrieval process whereby the learner reflects on and summarizes what has been learned. When left undone, between the time your students leave your class and the time they return to the next class, most of the information will have flown away. Hold on to that image.

EXIT TICKET

Revisit the success criteria associated with this chapter.

1. I can differentiate between learner performance and learning in the science classroom.

2. I can identify three cognitive principles that promote transfer and long-term learning.

3. I can explain the role of desirable difficulties in learning science.

Using the following Likert scales, reflect on and evaluate your own learning:

I can differentiate between learner performance and learning in the science classroom.

Got It   Getting There   Not Yet

Evidence:

I can identify three cognitive principles that promote transfer and long-term learning.

Got It   Getting There   Not Yet

Evidence:

I can explain the role of desirable difficulties in learning science.

Got It   Getting There   Not Yet

Evidence:

Now is the time for a few desirable difficulties of your own. Please complete the following chart about desirable difficulties. Some of the examples were presented in previous chapters. Now is the time to engage in spaced retrieval practice.

	WHAT IS THIS?	EXAMPLE FROM MY CLASSROOM OR THIS BOOK
Desirable difficulties		
Contrasting cases		
Analogies		
Concept maps		
The spacing effect		
Retrieval practice		

CHAPTER 8

The View From the Boat
Supporting the Journey From Snorkeling to Scuba Diving

Learning Intention

I understand my role in fostering and nurturing learner interest and engagement in K–5 science that results in higher-order thinking and deep conceptual understanding.

Success Criterion

By the end of this chapter, the following success criterion will be met:

1. I can develop a plan for determining my impact on student learning in my classroom.

FROM SNORKELING TO SCUBA DIVING

We presented the instructional framework that promotes *higher-order thinking and deep conceptual understanding* in the K–5 science classroom using a standards-based approach.

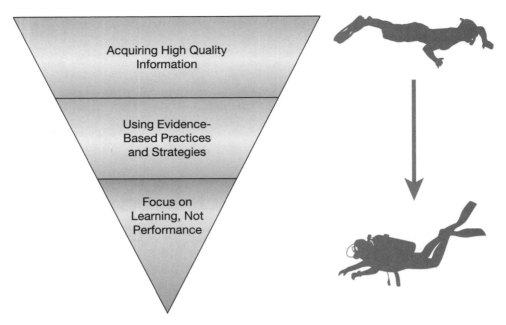

This framework, based on the research into how students learn, fosters and nurtures young learners' journey from snorkeling to scuba diving in science (See Markman, 2012). A strong body of research supports the conclusion that, as teachers, the decisions we make in classrooms matter a lot (Hattie, 2012). *It really is the teacher, dang it!* This is the first takeaway from this book: *We, as classroom teachers, can provide experiences that foster, nurture, and sustain deep cognitive engagement.* We began our own journey by unpacking the snorkeling and scuba diving metaphor, extracting the second main idea: *In our classrooms, there are snorkelers, and there are scuba divers.* Are you now able to compare and contrast snorkelers and scuba divers in your classroom?

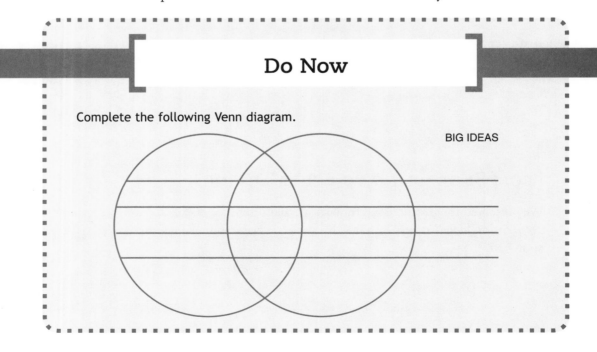

Do Now

Complete the following Venn diagram.

BIG IDEAS

Next, we explored how learning progresses through surface-level, deep-level, and then deep conceptual understanding. This is the learning progression for our young learners as they snorkel and scuba dive. This progression is all about thinking. Instead of focusing on labels, student background, and demographic characteristics, we should devote our time and energy to student thinking. *The SOLO Taxonomy is the framework for the journey from snorkeler to scuba diver.*

The first component of the instructional framework is that young learners must acquire high quality information. Emphasizing a standards-based approach, we experienced the process of identifying the priority standards in elementary science and how to unpack those standards, readying them for instruction. Using the model developed by Larry Ainsworth (2003, 2010), the chapter modeled the process using the Next Generation Science Standards. A particular area of focus for this chapter was that standards tell us *what* to teach, not *how*, so teachers can effectively guide students from snorkelers to scuba divers. Teachers must know exactly what to teach so the how and the what are perfectly aligned. *Unpacking the standards allows us to differentiate what students **need** to know from what is simply **neat** to know.*

This also requires us to build and activate background knowledge. *We must use prior knowledge and, at the same time, identify where additional background knowledge is needed for each learner to successfully dive into the new learning.*

The second component of the instructional framework is the use of evidence-based practices and strategies for teaching and learning K–5 science. This includes both models of instruction and specific learning strategies. Once you have clearly determined *what* you and the students are aiming for, you must identify the most appropriate and effective model of instruction and evidence-based strategies. These two chapters presented, discussed, and modeled various approaches to instruction by focusing on how *the what* from the previous chapters guides and informs this instructional decision: the *how*. *We must ensure that our approach to instruction matches the type of thinking we are striving for in our learners.*

The final component of the framework is providing opportunities for young learners to apply their learning to different contexts. What has been suggested in the research on higher-order thinking and transfer is that these are teachable traits or skills. That is, teachers can and do create educational environments that promote *higher-order thinking and deep conceptual understanding* in the K–5 science classroom. A significant component of this chapter included an explicit connection between the science of learning and *evidence-based practices. Teaching for transfer, regardless of whether the learning intention is for near or far transfer requires intentional and purposeful learning experiences and a focus on just that, learning, and not simply performance.*

Eight Main Ideas

1. *We, as classroom teachers, can provide experiences that foster, nurture, and sustain deep cognitive engagement.*
2. *In our classrooms, there are snorkelers, and there are scuba divers.*
3. *The SOLO Taxonomy is the framework for the journey from snorkeler to scuba diver.*
4. *Unpacking the standards allows us to differentiate what students need to know from what is simply neat to know.*
5. *We must use prior knowledge and, at the same time, identify where additional background knowledge is needed for each learner to successfully dive into the new learning.*
6. *We must ensure that our approach to instruction matches the type of thinking we are striving for in our learners.*
7. *Alignment between emotional, cognitive, and behavioral engagement and evidence-based strategies is required in the successful progression from snorkeler to scuba diver.*
8. *Teaching for transfer, regardless of whether the learning intention is for near or far transfer, requires intentional and purposeful learning experiences and a focus on just that, learning, and not simply performance.*

THE SNORKELING TO SCUBA DIVING CLASSROOM

What does this look like in today's classrooms? Meet Katy Campbell, Brittany Dunham, Annamarie Frost, Courtney Peckham, and Katherine Stevey. These five elementary teachers exemplify what the snorkeling to scuba diving classroom looks like with 21st-century learners. As you read their insight into promoting *higher-order thinking and deep conceptual understanding* in the K–5 science classroom, look back through the previous chapters, and match specific concepts with the real-world examples from these five classrooms.

VIGNETTE BOX

KATY CAMPBELL

I use a variety of strategies to keep students engaged in learning. I strive to first engage them emotionally by always starting lessons with an authentic hook, whether it is a video or some sort of concrete activity. For example, one of my favorite videos is one showing sound being visualized as a start to the sound unit: http://nigelstanford.com/Cymatics. Together, we watch this video at the beginning of the unit as a hook. I ask my students to engage in a brainstorming activity and discussion to elicit and activate prior knowledge. The video then serves as an anchor for later topics by watching it several times throughout the unit, after we have discussed pitch, frequency, and parts of a wave. I ask my students to analyze how the video represents these elements. I have also created a model of a cell using Jell-O (cytoplasm), a pedometer or other small electronic devices (nucleus), gummies (vacuoles), and a plastic bag (cell membrane) to give my students a concrete representation of a cell. As often as possible, we continue to explore our science concepts in a hands-on, minds-on way, whether by making instruments to explore change in pitch, doing science experiments with matter, or exploring rocks and minerals to develop classification rules. I also reinforce and promote the retrieval of all science concepts learned and buy myself time for more hands-on, minds-on tasks by integrating science into a literacy block. I use the science-based texts, or leveled readers on science concepts, during reading group rotations as my nonfiction texts concurrent with our science units to reinforce science vocabulary and concepts, to give students more examples and exposure, and to teach nonfiction text skills through something the students will have background knowledge in from my science lessons.

I think the hands-on, minds-on, highly visual activities and the science literacy work best for my learners. These lessons allow kids to grapple with a concept themselves, thus allowing them to authentically engage with the material by looking at the features of a rock or creating a change of state to better understand how that happens. The experiences also make the lesson emotionally engaging and thus more memorable. The visual activities (i.e., video, getting to play with the fake Jell-O cell) let them see a practical application of what they are learning and to apply their knowledge to different contexts. The science literacy reinforces concepts through frequent, spread out exposure to ideas. Plus, learning should be integrated. Reading about science makes reading more authentic and shows that ideas do not exist in separate silos.

Authentic experiences, such as making instruments or using mirrors to bounce laser pointers to hit a target, require students to apply what they learn in science in different contexts. If I say to build an instrument with a high pitch, then they have to understand that smaller instruments that vibrate faster will have a higher pitch. Or, if I give them a mirror and a laser and tell them to hit a target, they have to know that the light will reflect at the same angle with which it hits and how to position themselves accordingly. Plus, this kind of lesson promotes problem solving.

(Continued)

(Continued)

I think my favorite and most successful teaching experience was a series of sound exploration centers. Students rotated through four centers to discover different things about sound. They used a can to make sounds and thus discovered that sound came from vibrations. They had "mystery containers" filled with items to shake and attempt to guess the sounds. There were a series of rubber band instruments for students to play with to determine that the smaller "string" produces the higher sound. Then, they could loosen and tighten the rubber band to see how that changed the speed of vibration. Lastly, they dropped various objects and recorded the sound of impact to explore amplitude (energy of sound) and absorption of sound. This series of centers was entirely student-centered with me only walking around to prompt thinking with the occasional "why did _____ happen?" or "what would change if you did _____?" The students came away excited and eager to explore more sounds on their own. I felt like my students achieved flow, that elusive moment when the learning happens without the teacher and true inquiry arises. They were scuba divers!

BRITTANY DUNHAM

To foster, nurture, and sustain my students' engagement in science, I take every opportunity to make the learning interactive. Science is a subject that is meant for experiencing and testing. In Social Studies, students often have a more difficult time experiencing the topic being taught because they cannot place themselves back in 1776. With science, the students can ask questions, conduct experiments, and see firsthand why things are the way they are in the world. When students are able to have concrete, authentic experiences with friction, inertia, and electricity, for example, they are more likely to learn and also develop more questions, which as teachers, we should be striving for in young learners.

In my classroom, giving students choices is often a top strategy. When students have choices in how they engage with their learning, young learners are going to be more vested in the content and feel that their perspectives and experiences are valued in the classroom. Too often, I think teachers feel a need to completely control the room, control the lessons, and control the grades. Why can't we have students choose some aspects of these elements? As an adult, when I am given a choice as to how I want to do things, I am apt to be happier and likely to have a better attitude about the experience. When students have a choice of how to show what they know, where they want to do the work, and what thinking processes they want to use, they feel a sense of ownership in the learning. If a student feels valued by a teacher, he or she is more likely to take risks to meet higher expectations.

Another strategy that works for me is cooperative learning. I find true value in students working together to learn from each other but also to collaboratively discover new content. Sometimes a student who is misunderstanding a topic can find clarity by hearing the explanation from a peer. In other cases, a student who has more knowledge on a topic can be a great resource for a student who does not yet have that knowledge base. I often ask myself, "who is doing more talking, me or the students?" This question helps drive my teaching and challenges me to find ways to integrate cooperative learning, and dialogue, into my classroom.

In order to have students engage in higher-order thinking, I encourage students to be the teacher. Again, when I am lesson planning, I try to ask myself, "who is doing more talking, me or the kids?" In class, I strive to give my students the background knowledge to be successful, but I also try to incorporate times for students to expand that breadth and depth of knowledge. My students are much more engaged when they know they are learning for a purpose! I have found students will learn so much more if we give them the opportunities to integrate their interests and passions with the content.

This year, I was teaching my students about potential and kinetic energy. Instead of showing them a picture of a roller coaster and highlighting examples of potential and kinetic energy, I gave them the chance to create their own roller coasters. I gave them the performance task that required them to complete their roller coaster in only 20 minutes and with a finite set of supplies. I have never seen so many actively engaged students working together! The students worked in pairs and constructed amazing roller coasters given their time limit. Each pair shared the points of the potential and kinetic energy and looked at other students' roller coasters. I loved that the students were working together during the activity but also that they found ways to make creatively designed roller coasters. There were flips, inverts, loops, and hills. If I had shown students a picture of a roller coaster, I am sure they would have thought it was neat, but seeing them construct one and having a say about how it looked reminded me how great an authentic experience is for promoting higher-order thinking. I was watching scuba divers in action.

ANNAMARIE FROST

I think that the key to engagement is varying the ways in which I teach science—which has changed dramatically since my first year in the classroom. I used to implement ALL whole group instruction, with a daily assessment, and a test at the end of the unit. We also only allotted 25-30 minutes per day for science. Now my classroom is very different. First off, we spend 45 minutes each day teaching

(Continued)

(Continued)

science content. My school was 1 of 10 in the district that took on a personalized learning initiative this year, and the focus has transformed my science teaching. We spend 1 day getting introduced to the topic, completing a Know-What-How-Learn (KWHL) chart, getting familiar with new vocabulary, and going over study guides that go home. Then we spend a few days working in small group stations exploring the topic using digital content (Discovery Education, BrainPop, etc.), collaborating with peers on tasks, and being led by a teacher through a performance assessment, activity, investigation, or experiment. Our district also has a bank of STEM projects, so when the units align, learners get that experience as well. They may not go smoothly, and the collaboration may not be 100% all of the time, but it's definitely the time when the students are most engaged in their learning. I get to take a step back and watch the learning occur, and I can step in to facilitate and coach the learning when needed.

Being in a school with a high English language learner (ELL) population, I rely heavily on classroom discussion using turn and talks. I can ask a question and give students time to discuss it with a partner before sharing their collective response out the group. I remember back last year when we were sorting predators and prey. My learners were having discussions identifying similarities and differences. This type of discussion on topics is worth having because some ambiguities in the concepts help the learner see that science is not always black and white. There's a lot of grey. In addition, I've found that doing small group investigations is much easier to manage than a whole group investigation. There are fewer variables that pull on learners' attention and cognitive load.

I've also found that science helps with contributing to the growth mindset that students need time developing early on in their educational trajectory. Learning from their mistakes to improve the next time is crucial. When scientists make a hypothesis about what *might* happen, they're rarely correct. When students make a hypothesis about how an investigation or experiment might go, it's initially hard for them to accept if their hypothesis isn't correct. But I've found it to be a teachable moment for students to take that hypothesis (whether it's correct or incorrect) and use it to have a stronger conclusion about where to go next.

Although we do have to give our students common assessments, they can't authentically reach the higher levels of the SOLO Taxonomy. Because of this, we have to intentionally find time to plan for experiments, investigations, STEM experiences, and project-based learning (PBL). Those are the times that students remember most of their learning, times when they're taking control of their learning, and I can step back and watch it happen. I also know that when students are choosing to integrate science topics (simple machines) into their indoor recess activities, they are truly enjoying their learning in science! I have to give them opportunities to do so.

My favorite teaching experience is the energy PBL that our grade-level team has done with our students for the past 2 years. One of my coworkers created it in the summer of 2015. The implementation of PBL has changed a lot from Year 1 to 2. This specific task is centered on our standards, specifically renewable energy sources and the advantages and disadvantages that come with them. Last year, we looked at 4 different regions around the country. This year we connected with a mapmaker from the county to gain access to bird's eye view maps of our school as well as three other schools in the district. Students were given the task to analyze the map and decide on the renewable energy source they thought the school should look into (water, sun, wind) and why. The project was completely cross-curricular—we studied *The Boy Who Harnessed the Wind* as a launch event during read aloud time, did research about energy sources during reading, wrote informational paragraphs and persuasive letters pertaining to renewable energy sources during writing, and assembled the project using display boards or Google slides during science. The students recorded the presentations to send to administrators of the schools we studied and invited community members to hear the presentations. Our learners had opportunities to reflect on their progress, and each school team from each class got to listen to each other's projects to compare and contrast their findings.

COURTNEY PECKHAM

The more hands-on and minds-on students can be with science content, the more I find they stay engaged. Students love seeing and feeling the content in front of them and getting to manipulate the materials used in science. I find that using an inquiry-based learning approach in science is most beneficial for students. When students come upon the answers themselves, or discover solutions on their own, not only do they feel accomplished, but they also take ownership in their discovery and their learning. I love allowing students to be as hands-on as possible throughout our science units. When students take ownership of their own learning, and discover the material on their own, they want to know more. This pride in their understanding leads them to ask higher-level questions and comprehend the material at a deeper level. Students in my classroom are always asked to question their thinking and connect it to other material. We build a culture that encourages failure and questioning, which allows students to feel comfortable thinking in a different or deeper way.

(Continued)

(Continued)

My best science teaching experience was adding a MakerSpace to my science instruction this year. This space has allowed students to build and create using their understanding of science and incorporate their creations into our science curriculum. Earlier this year, students made 3D ocean food webs that depicted the flow of energy through the use of a moving part. Watching students take their understanding of food webs and use it to create physical representations allowed me to see what they understood, as well as how far they could push their understanding of food webs. The MakerSpace has allowed me to differentiate my instruction during science and has really helped me to include the inquiry piece into my teaching.

KATHERINE STEVEY

Before the teaching starts, I always make sure to know where my students are coming from and to ask them what they want. I can do this in many ways. I begin each day by greeting each kid in every block by name at the door. I try to get them to look at me, so that they know that I am talking to them and that I see them. I compliment them and ask them questions. I find out a lot of things by doing this! Other ways I might find out what they are into are having them relate any content we will be discussing to their own lives and experiences, having them do simple thought inventories using Google Forms, or getting them to talk to their peers in work groups. A way to do this during or after a lesson is by using Kagan strategies for round table type thought processes or even as simple as giving me feedback or information on sticky notes they can "park" (anonymously or not) on the ozone poster in the back.

When I am planning a lesson, I feel very much like a salesperson or the hairdresser I used to be. I ask myself questions like, Who is the most important one? What do I want to accomplish? What do I need to be successful? Let's start by talking about the "who." Students are the most important "one" in the lesson. If I can get them to *want to do* what I have planned, then I have won the first battle. Now, there is a lot to be said for the level of buy-in you can get just by getting them to do it— this doesn't necessarily mean that they are "all in" for learning, living, and breathing it. They may just be gliding through it because it is how they get through the block and how they pass time in a school day. I have had moments where I realized this to be the case, so I reinvented myself about 100 times with the students as the central character of importance in the novel of my lesson. If they are the most important ones, then I want them to feel like there is nothing they would trade for the experience they are about to have in the 80-minute class period. Nothing. I believe in the basics: graphic organizers, notes, asking questions without giving the answers, conversations that lead to more questions, and more interest. Questions lead kids to want answers, which makes the learning automatically all about them. They are very into themselves! So, that is my first goal—to make sure that they leave our first minutes, or that day's lesson, with plenty of questions. I really feel that I have won this one many times over when a student goes home and e-mails me to tell me that they have found an answer and then typed a message to explain it to me! Another favorite is when they are so excited about knowing where to find an object in the night sky, or explain moon phases, that they go home and take everyone outside to show them.

The neat thing about questions is that if we are doing a Know-Want-Learn (KWL) for tides, for example, they might ask things like "what is a tide?," "what causes the tide?," "how big or small can tides be?"—these would cover the content learning about the gravitational pull of the sun and moon, the moon's position relative to the Earth and sun, neap and spring tides, and so on. But asking about how the tides affect the life of living things, or wanting to know if there are tides that exist anywhere else in the solar system, are questions that will lead children down a path to finding, or not finding, information that is *not the content* but rather the motivation for caring about the content since it satisfies their thirst for being all about themselves.

So, once they have asked the questions that lead to the lesson, I then hold their thirst over their heads, so to speak. The lessons commence, but I make sure to build in time for their own research and have a research rubric for each unit that is, again, all about them. They can choose a topic related to the topic of the unit and do research to produce a product that is shared with the class. They can build models, make brochures or posters, write papers, or create a PowerPoint or a Prezi presentation. I not only build in time daily, but weekly try to carve out at least half a block on Fridays for them to work, so that no one is trying to do something at home without the tools they need. There is a level playing field, and everyone has access to the same opportunities and materials, resources, and technology. They begin by writing a proposal, telling me what they want to find out, how they intend to find it out, what product they will make, and why it is important to them. I sign off on proposals, then they just beg me to do it. In my mind, the projects are kind of like the whole point, and as we are doing the learning and I know what they are working on, I can relate the content to the ideas they are currently working on. This process is very fluid, and we come back to asking questions constantly and talking about the content as a result. Also, it motivates them to do just about anything I ask. They will often ask me if there is going to be built in research time that day, and I am always skeptical, like, "We have a lot to get done, so you are going to need to really focus on our goals for today." I never make it sound like a sure thing. It is special to get that time and special indeed to see the results. Are there kids who struggle to meet a lessons

(Continued)

(Continued)

objective? Yes, and the beautiful thing is that I can remediate and reteach during that time if needed. Likewise, for a gifted group, they likely know the content already, so getting them to buy in can be challenging. Their instinct is to check out, but I won't let them. As soon as they are on fire for their own approved interests, beautiful things happen!

On higher level thinking—I don't start a unit lesson on the planets where I want kids to know the composition of planets and their order by telling them the composition of the planets and their order. They may or may not remember the planets, so we might use a roundtable Kagan-type activity to get them to remember them, then do research and collect data on all of the planets, such as position relative to the sun, diameter, composition, distance, high and low temperatures, atmosphere composition, and so on. I recently did this with collaborative groups researching a planet, creating simple posters with all of the information, and then gallery walks so that everyone was able to get the information they needed. Then I had them make decisions about how we could categorize the planets. I asked them, "what would the headers be?" They came up with these categories across groups the last time: by size, by distance from the sun, whether or not they had rings, whether or not they tended to have moons, rocky or gas, and atmosphere or no atmosphere. They were great conversations, student-centered activities, and I never had to "tell" them the content. They were in the driver's seat, deciding what was important or not. They liked that a lot.

My best moments in teaching science happen so often that I am not sure I could say there is any one thing that made something good from my perspective. I reflect daily, and I take student feedback seriously. I talked earlier about how students are egocentric little beings and like things to be all about them. It is funny, because I also strive to give them a little bit of the idea that there really is nothing so unique about any of us. There are millions more just like them, with similar ideas, questions, and interests. It is getting them to step away from themselves and realize that the difference they make isn't going to be so much about them as it is other people, that brings the greatest satisfaction. When they are racing home to talk about what they are learning in science, and then racing back to tell me about it, they are going beyond their own self-interest and touching younger and older siblings, parents, neighbors, and a kid on the bus with an excitement that means we had a great lesson. One of the most satisfying moments this year came when students returned from asking people why they thought the way the moon looked changed throughout a month. They asked anyone they could find and took anecdotal notes. Most people, young or old, could not tell them. They were instructed not to affirm any answer or explain their own thinking or understanding.

This gave us the most fantastic opportunity to discuss and list all of the misconceptions people have about something so simple! Rather than have me find out the misconceptions, they found them out firsthand and contributed them to our class discussion. There was much greater meaning in this, and we came back to those foundational misunderstandings again and again throughout that unit. ∎

MAKING YOUR OWN JOURNEY FROM A SNORKELER TO SCUBA DIVER

So, what next? How do we change our practice and adjust our instructional decisions to maximize the learning in our science classrooms? Changing our own practice is successful only when we reflect on our own journey from snorkeling to scuba diving and, along with our students, see ourselves as learners. In order to change our practice, we first need to gain insights into what **we** want to change.

Do Now

Take some time and reflect on your own strengths and areas where you need opportunities for growth. Use the following table to summarize your thoughts. In the column on the right, share several areas of strength and also areas where you need growth opportunities. ∎

	STRENGTH OR OPPORTUNITY
1. Using the SOLO Taxonomy to better understand my learners' thinking	
2. Unpacking the standards to be certain I know what learners need to know, understand, and be able to do	
3. Activating my learners' prior knowledge	
4. Building my learners' background knowledge	
5. Selecting a model of instruction that matches the type of thinking expected of my students	
6. Using evidence-based strategies that engage my learners	
7. Teaching for transfer by focusing on learning and not just performance	

For the items that you indicated were strengths in the previous Do-Now Box, provide a specific example from your teaching that would support your assertion that the item is indeed a strength. What evidence would you point to in your classroom to support such assertions? If you cannot identify a specific example, then change your response from a strength to an opportunity.

Do Now

	STRENGTH OR OPPORTUNITY	EVIDENCE OR SPECIFIC EVIDENCE
1. Using the SOLO Taxonomy to better understand my learners' thinking		
2. Unpacking the standards to be certain I know what learners need to know, understand, and be able to do		
3. Activating my learners' prior knowledge		
4. Building my learners' background knowledge		
5. Selecting a model of instruction that matches the type of thinking expected of my students		
6. Using evidence-based strategies that engage my learners		
7. Teaching for transfer by focusing on learning and not just performance		

When we include a chart like the previous one as part of our reflective practice, it requires that we have a consistent system of self-reflection on what is happening in our classrooms. This data chart can guide conversations with our instructional leaders, mentors, or colleagues. "Know thy impact" is an essential component of *Visible Learning* and requires self-reflection (Hattie, 2012). The strengths are to provide the foundation for changing practice by identifying successes. The opportunities become the focus for changing our practice. Each opportunity becomes an area of focus.

Now, convert each opportunity into a goal with success criteria for yourself. For example, if you identify that you use too much "sit and get" lecture or packets, then your goal or success criteria might be *to increase the number of opportunities for classroom discussion and dialogue in student learning* (see Chapter 6). It is important to have a clear understanding of what success looks like to better identify resources and supports for implementing your goal and monitoring your progress. In other words, what are the success criteria for this goal? An example is found in the following table.

GOAL	*I will increase the number of opportunities for classroom discussion and dialogue in student learning.*
SUCCESS CRITERIA	1. I will incorporate two or more opportunities for classroom discussion into the learning period. 2. I will monitor student discussion to better assess student understanding. 3. I will use data from classroom discussions to plan the next step in the learning episode. 4. I will collaborate with my planning team to develop opportunities for classroom discussion.

Do Now

Select one of your opportunities and develop a goal and success criteria for that opportunity. Use the ideas in previous chapters to select your specific goal. ∎

GOAL	*I will*
SUCCESS CRITERIA	1. 2. 3. 4.

This exercise will support your effectiveness in making conscious decisions about what professional learning is necessary to enhance the probability that you will achieve your targeted goal and success criteria. As highlighted by Timperely, Wilson, Barrar, and Fung (2007), this professional learning should do the following:

1. Occur over an extended period of time as learning takes time: This goal will not be mastered by Friday.

2. Challenge your existing beliefs: Rather than looking for evidence that you are right, look for evidence that your strategy did not work.

3. Encourage dialogue amongst colleagues.

4. Garner support from school leadership.

It is extremely important that we dialogue among colleagues, gather support from school leadership, take every opportunity to observe effective classroom instruction, and participate in a professional learning community (PLC) with teachers who practice visible learning. This gives you an opportunity to gather specific feedback on your progress toward the goals and success criteria you have established. Every hallway conversation, teachers' lounge discussion, or classroom observation about learning is an opportunity for feedback.

As you move forward in this reflective process, you will begin to focus on the evidence of your impact in changing teacher practice and thus student learning. After all, shouldn't we model the very learning we expect from our students?

AND NEXT, THERE'S JACKSON

At the very beginning of this book, you met Tessa, John's inquisitive five-year-old daughter. She has a little brother named Jackson. At two years old, Jackson is quickly following in his sister's footsteps.

Don't get me wrong, Jackson is his own person. What I mean is that Jackson has quickly picked up the skill of asking questions and exploring his world. At age two, his favorite question is, "What's dat [that], daddy?" Tessa has taken him under her wing and provided him engaging experiences that promote higher-order thinking and deep conceptual understanding in *life*. Jackson loves talking with his sister about the worm farm on our front porch and the amazing things you can do with sand.

The point we are trying to make is that Tessa and Jackson possess an inspiring level of curiosity for how the world works. Although they are far from being little scientists, these two young learners are already snorkeling and scuba diving on a daily basis. Jackson has developed surface knowledge of how certain things in his world, as well as the world of his sister, work. That surface knowledge has paralleled his growth in understanding process skills for acquiring and encoding experiences, interactions, and vocabulary. This foundation provides the necessary prior knowledge and background knowledge for deep learning and transfer. As he moves toward his third birthday, he has already started to uncover relationships between light and shadows; the needs of living things; and the sun, Earth, moon, and stars, as well as the highly abstract idea of gravity and the motion of objects. What we hope to have conveyed in the previous chapters is that the classroom should nurture and sustain this incredible

growth, development, and, thus, learning. Do you remember the following question from the Introduction of this book? Try it again.

❓ QUESTION BOX

At what point does research say that children stop asking questions in school?

(a) Elementary School: Kids learn that teachers value right answers more than a provocative question.

(b) High School: Teenagers become absorbed in other matters relevant to their social world, such as a text message, and interpreting what it means.

(c) Never: Curiosity is an innate feature of the brain. ∎

Yes, there are right and wrong answers. However, in the learning journey of our young learners, don't take away their scuba gear, don't send them into the water without enough oxygen, and don't separate them from their diving buddies and make them dive on their own. As you look into the water from the boat, don't leave their diving experience to chance, preoccupied with distractions above the surface of the water. And certainly, don't let them come to learn that snorkeling is the best way to see the world.

FROM SNORKELERS TO SCUBA DIVERS IN THE ELEMENTARY SCIENCE CLASSROOM

Each and every day, young learners enter our classrooms, diving gear in hand, with a variety of experiences that have shaped their background and prior knowledge, the nature of their thinking, and the nature of their interactions. Divers may have different diving gear, but what they have is the starting point for their next adventure. Our jobs are to take that gear and, together, get it ready for a successful diving experience, not spend our time criticizing their gear. They brought what they had available to them, and we should applaud them for showing up at all. Now, give them a diving experience they won't forget. Tessa, Jackson, and their classmates are counting on you!

EXIT TICKET

Development of a

PERSONAL ACTION PLAN

Given what I now know about engaging the brain, what will I do next or do differently in my classroom?

1.

2.

3.

4.

5.

Where will I look for support in implementing these ideas?

_____

_____

_____

_____

_____

_____

_____

_____

_____

_____

_____

_____

_____

_____

_____

References

Abrami, P. C., Bernard, R. M., Borokhovski, E., Waddington, D. I., Wade, C. A., & Persson, T. (2015). Strategies for teaching students to think critically: A meta-analysis. *Review of Educational Research, 85*(2), pp. 275–314.

Adams, G. L., & Engelmann, S. (1996). *Research on direct instruction: 25 Years beyond Distar.* Seattle, WA: Educational Achievement Systems.

Ainsworth, L. (2003). *"Unwrapping" the standards: A simple process to make standards* manageable. Englewood, CO: Lead + Learn Press.

Ainsworth, L. (2010). *Rigorous curriculum design: How to create curricular units of study that align standards, instruction, and assessment.* Englewood, CO: Lead + Learn Press.

Alexander, R.J. (2017). *Towards dialogic teaching: Rethinking classroom talk* (5th ed.). Cambridge, MA: Dialogos.

Alexander, P. A., Kulikowich, J. M., & Jetton, T. L. (1994). The role of subject-matter knowledge and interest in the processing of linear and nonlinear texts. *Review of Educational Research, 64,* 201–252.

Alexander, P. A., Kulikowich, J. M., & Jetton, T. L. (1995). Interrelationship of knowledge, interest, and recall: Assessing a model of domain learning. *Journal of Educational Psychology, 87*(4), 559–575.

Allen, R. H. (2001). *Impact teaching: Ideas and strategies for teachers to maximize student learning.* Boston, MA: Allyn & Bacon.

Almarode, J. T. (2011*). Frequency, duration, and time devoted to elementary science instruction and the association with science achievement and science interest* (Doctoral dissertation). Retrieved from Online Archive of University of Virginia Scholarship.

Almarode, J. T., & Miller, A. M. (2013). *Captivate, activate, and invigorate the student brain in math and science grades 6–12.* Thousand Oaks, CA: Corwin.

Alvermann, D. (1981). The compensatory effect of graphic organizers on descriptive texts. *Journal of Educational Research, 75,* 44–48.

Anderson, J. R. (1983). *The architecture of cognition.* Cambridge, MA: Harvard University Press.

Anderson, L. W., & Sosniak, L. A. (Eds.). (1994). *Bloom's taxonomy: A forty-year perspective.* Chicago, IL: University of Chicago Press.

Antonetti, J., & Garver, J. (2015). *17,000 classroom visits can't be wrong.* Alexandria, VA: Association for Supervision and Curriculum Development.

Appleton, J., Christenson, S., & Furlong, M. (2008). Student engagement with school: Critical conceptual and methodological issues of the construct. *Psychology in the Schools, 45*, 369–386.

Appleton, J., Christenson, S., Kim, D., & Reschly, A. (2006). Measuring cognitive and psychological engagement: Validation of the Student Engagement Instrument. *Journal of School Psychology, 44*, 427–445.

Ausubel, D. P. (1968). *Educational psychology: A cognitive view*. New York, NY: Holt, Rinehart & Winston.

Bahrick, H. P. (2000). Long-term maintenance of knowledge. In E. Tulving & F. I. M. Craik (Eds.), *The Oxford handbook of memory* (pp. 347–362). New York, NY: Oxford Press.

Baniflower, E., Cohen, K., Pasley, J., & Weiss, I. (2008). *Effective science instruction: What does research tell us?* Portsmouth, NH: RMC Research Corporation, Center on Instruction.

Bennett, S., Maton, K., & Kervin, L. (2008). The 'digital natives' debate: A critical review of the evidence. *British Journal of Educational Technology, 39*(5), 775–786.

Biggs, J. B., & Collis, K. F. (1982). *Evaluating the quality of learning: The SOLO taxonomy (structure of observed learning outcome)*. New York, NY: Academic Press.

Birkerts, S. (1994). *The Gutenberg elegies: The fate of reading in an electronic age*. Boston, MA: Faber and Faber.

Bjork, R. A. (1994). Memory and metamemory considerations in the training of human beings. In J. Metcalfe & A. Shimamura (Eds.), *Metacognition: Knowing about knowing* (pp. 185–205). Cambridge, MA: MIT.

Bjork, E. L., & Bjork, R. A. (2014). Making things hard on yourself, but in a good way: Creating desirable difficulties to enhance learning. In M. A. Gernsbacher & J. Pomerantz (Eds.), *Psychology and the real world: Essays illustrating fundamental contributions to society*, 2nd edition (pp. 60–68). New York, NY: Worth.

Bloom, B., Englehart, M., Furst, E., Hill., & Krothwohl, D. (1956). *Taxonomy of educational objects: The classification of educational goals. Handbook I: Cognitive domain.* New York, NY: McKay.

Boaler, J. (1998). Open and closed mathematics: Student experiences and understandings. *Journal for Research in Mathematics Education, 29*(1), 41–62.

Boulanger, F. D. (1981). Instruction and science learning: A quantitative synthesis. *Journal of Research in Science Teaching, 18*(4), 311–327.

Bransford, J., Brown, A., & Cocking, R. (Eds.). (2000). *How people learn, expanded version.* Washington, DC: National Academies Press.

Brualdi, A. C. (1998). *Classroom questions: ERIC/AE Digest*, ERIC Digest Series No. EDO-TM-98–02, Los Angeles, CA: ERIC Clearinghouse for Community Colleges, University of California at Los Angeles.

Carr, N. G. (2010). *The shallows: What the Internet is doing to our brains.* New York, NY: Norton.

Cazden, C. (2001). *Classroom discourse: The language of teaching and learning.* Portsmouth, NH: Heinemann.

Cepeda, N. J., Pashler, H., Vul, E., Wixted, J. T., & Rohrer, D. (2006). Distributed practice in verbal recall tasks: A review and quantitative synthesis. *Psychological Bulletin, 132*, 354–380.

Chambers, D.W. (1983). Stereotypic images of the scientist: The Draw a Scientist Test. *Science Education. 67*(2): 255–265.

Corno, L. (1993). The best–laid plans: Modern conceptions of volition and educational research. *Educational Researcher, 22* (2), 14–22.

Craik, F. I. M. (2002). Levels of processing: Past, present . . . and future? *Memory, 10*, 305–318.

Craik, F. I. M., & Lockhart, R. S. (1972). Levels of processing: A framework for memory research. *Journal of Verbal Learning and Verbal Behavior, 11*, 671–684.

Craik, F. I. M., & Tulving, E. (1975). Depth of processing and the retention of words in episodic memory. *Journal of Experimental Psychology: General, 104*, 268–294.

Dantonio, M., & Beisenherz, P. (2001). *Learning to question, questioning to learn.* Boston, MA: Allyn & Bacon.

Darr, C. W. (2012). Measuring student engagement: The development of a scale for formative use. In S. L. Christenson, A. Reschly, & C. Wyle (Eds.), *Handbook of research on student engagement* (pp. 707–723). New York, NY: Springer.

Dohrenwend, B. S. (1965). Some effects of open and closed questions on respondents' answers. *Human Organization, 24*(2), 175–184.

Donovan, S., & Bransford, J. (eds.). (2005). *How students learn: Science in the classroom.* Washington, DC: National Academies Press.

Driver, R., Squires, A., Rushworth, P., & Wood-Robinson. (2005). *Making sense of secondary science: Research into children's ideas.* New York, NY: Routledge.

Duncan, G. J., Dowsett, C. J., Claessens, A., Magnuson, K., Hutson, A. C., Klebanov, P., . . . Japel, C. (2007). School readiness and later achievement. *Developmental Psychology, 43*(6), 1428–1446.

Durso, F. T., & Coggins, K. A. (1991). Organized instruction for the improvement of word knowledge skills. *Journal of Educational Psychology, 83*(1), 108–112.

Duschl, R. A., & Osborne, J. (2002). Supporting and promoting argumentation discourse in science education. *Studies in Science Education, 38*, 39–72.

Estes, T. H., Mills, D. C., & Barron, R. F. (1969). Three methods of introducing students to a reading-learning task in two content subjects. In H. L. Herber & P. L. Sanders (Eds.), *Research in reading in the content areas: First year report* (pp. 40–47). Syracuse, NY: Syracuse University Press.

Estes, T. H., & Mintz, S. (2015). *Instruction: A models approach* (7th ed.). Boston, MA: Pearson.

Fredericks, J. A., Blumenfeld, P. C., & Paris, A. H. (2004). School engagement: Potential of the concept, state of the evidence. *Review of Educational Research, 74*(1), 49–109.

Finn, J. (1989). Withdrawing from school. *Review of Educational Research, 59*, 117–142.

Finn, J. (1993). *School engagement and students at risk.* Washington, DC: National Center for Educational Statistics.

Finn, J., & Voelkl, K. (1993). School characteristics related to school engagement. *The Journal of Negro Education, 62*, 249–268.

Finson, K. D. (2002). Drawing a scientist: What we do and do not know after fifty years of drawings. *School Science and Mathematics, 102*(7), 335–345.

Fischer, T. A., & Tarver, S. G. (1997). Meta-analysis of studies of mathematics curricula design around big ideas. *Effective School Practices, 16*, 71–79.

Foos, P. W. (1995). The effect of variations in text summarization opportunities on test performance. *Journal of Experimental Education, 63*, 89–95.

Forness, S. R., Kavale, K. A., Blum, I. M., & Lloyd, J. W. (1997). Mega-analysis of meta-analyses. *Teaching Exceptional Children, 29(6)*, 4–9.

Griffin, M. M., & Robinson, D. H. (2005). Does spatial or visual information in maps facilitate text recall? Reconsidering the conjoint retention hypothesis. *Educational Technology Research and Development, 53*, 23–36.

Hasher, L., & Zacks, R. T. (1984a). Automatic and effortful processes in memory. *Journal of Experimental Psychology, 198*, 356–388.

Hasher, L., & Zacks, R. T. (1984b). Automatic processing of fundamental information: The case for frequency of occurrence. *American Psychologist, 39*, 1372–1388.

Hattie, J. (2009). *Visible learning: A synthesis of over 800 meta-analyses relating to achievement.* New York, NY: Routledge.

Hattie, J. (2012). *Visible learning for teachers: Maximizing impact on learning.* New York, NY: Routledge.

Hattie, J., Fisher, D., & Frey, N. (2017). *Visible learning for mathematics. What works best to optimize student learning.* Thousand Oaks, CA: Corwin.

Holliday, W. G., Brunner, L. L., & Donais, E. L. (1977). Differential cognitive and affective responses to flow diagrams in science. *Journal of Research in Science Teaching, 14*, 129–138.

Hook, P., & Mills, J. (2011). *SOLO taxonomy: A guide for schools. Book 1.* United Kingdom: Essential Resources Educational Publishers Limited.

Hook, P., & Mills, J. (2012). *SOLO taxonomy: A guide for schools. Book 2.* United Kingdom: Essential Resources Educational Publishers Limited.

Horton, P. B., McConney, A. A., Gallo, M., Woods, A. L., Senn, G. J., & Hamelin, D. (1993). An investigation of the effectiveness of concept mapping as an instructional tool. *Science Education, 77*, 95–111.

Ives, B., & Hoy, C. (2003). Graphic organizers applied to higher-level secondary mathematics. *Learning Disabilities Research & Practice, 18*, 36–51.

Johnson, D. W., & Johnson, R. T. (1999). Making cooperative learning work. *Theory Into Practice, 38*(2), 67–73.

Kagan, S. (1989). *The structural approach to cooperative learning.* Alexandria, VA: Association for Supervision and Curriculum Development.

King, A. (1994). Guiding knowledge construction in the classroom: Effects of teaching children how to question and how to explain. *American Educational Research Journal, 31*(2), 338–368.

Kirby, J., & Biggs, J. (1981). *Cognitive abilities, students' learning processes and academic achievement.* Final Report to Australian Research Grants Committee: Canberra.

Klahr, D., & Nigam, M. (2004). The equivalence of learning paths in early science instruction: Effects of direct instruction and discovery learning. *Psychological Science, 15,* 661–667.

Krathwohl, D. R. (2002). A revision of Bloom's taxonomy: An overview. *Theory Into Practice, 41*(4), 212–218.

La Paro, K. M., & Pianta, R. C. (2000). Predicting children's competence in the early school years: A meta-analytic review. *Review of Educational Research, 70*(4), 443–484.

LeDoux, J. (2002). *Synaptic self: How our brains become who we are.* New York, NY: Viking Press.

Leslie, I. (2014). *Curious. The desire to know and why your future depends on it.* New York, NY: Basic Books.

Litman, J. A., Hutchins, T. L., & Russon, R. K. (2005). Epistemic curiosity, feeling-of-knowing, and exploratory behaviour. *Cognition and Emotion, 19(4),* 559–582.

Loewenstein, G. (1994). The psychology of curiosity: A review and reinterpretation. *Psychological Bulletin, 116*(1), 75–98.

Maltese, A. V., & Tai, R. H. (2010). Eyeballs in the fridge: Sources of early interest in science. *International Journal of Science Education, 32,* 669–685.

Markman, A. (2012). *Smart thinking. Three essential keys to solve problems, innovate, and get things done.* New York, NY: Penguin Group.

Marks, H. M. (2000). Student engagement in instructional activity: Patterns in elementary, middle, and high school years. *American Educational Research Journal, 37,* 153–184.

Martin, S. (2012). *Using SOLO as a framework for teaching.* United Kingdom: Essential Resources Educational Publishers Limited.

Marzano, R. J. (2001). *Designing a new taxonomy of educational objectives.* Thousand Oaks, CA: Corwin.

Marzano, R. J. (2004). *Building background knowledge for acacdemic achievement. Research on what works in schools.* Alexandria, VA: Association for Supervision and Curriculum Development.

Marzano, R. J., & Pickering, D. J. (2005). *Building academic vocabulary teacher's manual.* Alexandria, VA: Association for Supervision and Curriculum Development.

Marzano, R. J., Pickering, D. J., & Heflebower, T. (2010). *The highly engaged classroom.* Bloomington, IN: Solution Tree Press.

Marzano, R. J., Pickering, D. J., & Pollock, J. E. (2001). *Classroom instruction that works: Research-based strategies for increasing student achievement.* Alexandria, VA: ASCD.

Mayer, R. E., (2003). The promise of multimedia learning: Using the same instructional design methods across different media. *Learning and Instruction, 13*(2), 125–139.

Mayer, R. E. (2011). *Applying the science of learning.* New York, NY: Pearson.

McPeck, J. (1981). *Critical thinking and education.* Toronto, Ontario, Canada: Oxford University Press.

Medina, J. (2014a). *Brain rules for baby. How to raise a smart and happy child from zero to five* (2nd ed.). Seattle, WA: Pear Press.

Medina, J. (2014b). *Brain rules. 12 principles for surviving and thriving at work, home, and school.* Seattle, WA: Pear Press.

Meehan, H. (1979). *Learning lessons.* Cambridge, MA: Harvard University Press.

Mercer, N., & Littleton, K. (2007). *Dialogue and the development of children's thinking.* London, UK: Routledge.

Minstrell, J. (1989). Teaching science for understanding. In L.B. Resnick and L.E. Klopfer (Eds.), *Toward the thinking curriculum: Current cognitive research* (pp. 129–149). Alexandria, VA: Association for Supervision and Curriculum Development.

National Research Council. (2012). *A framework for K-12 science education: Practices, cross-cutting concepts, and core ideas.* Washington, DC: National Academies Press.

National Science Board. (2007). *National action plan for addressing the critical needs of the U.S. science, technology, engineering, and mathematics education system.* Arlington, VA: National Science Foundation.

Nesbit, J. C., & Adesope, O. O. (2006). Learning with concept and knowledge maps: A meta-analysis. *Review of Educational Research, 76*(3), 413–448.

Newton, P., Driver, R., & Osborne, J. (1999). The place of argumentation in the pedagogy of school science. *International Journal of Science Education, 21*(5), 553–576.

NGSS Lead States. (2013). *Next generation science standards: For states, by states.* Washington, DC: The National Academies Press.

Novak, J. D., & Gowin, D. B. (1984). *Learning how to learn.* New York, NY: Cambridge University Press.

O'Donnell, A. M., Dansereau, D. F., & Hall, R. H. (2002). Knowledge maps as scaffolds for cognitive processing. *Educational Psychology Review, 14*, 71–86.

Patterson M. E., Dansereau, D. F., & Wiegmann, D. A. (1993). Receiving information during a cooperative episode: Effects of communication aids and verbal ability. *Learning and Individual Differences 5*, 1–11.

Perkins, D. N., & Salomon, G. (1992). *Transfer of learning. Contribution to the International Encyclopedia of Education* (2nd ed.). Oxford, UK: Pergamon Press.

Pintrich, P. (2004). A conceptual framework for assessing motivation and self-regulated learning in college students. *Educational Psychology Review, 16*, 385–407.

Pressley, M., Harris, K. R., & Marks, M. B. (1992). But good strategy instructors are constructivists! *Educational Psychology Review, 4*, 3–31.

Pusateri, T. P. (2003). *Instructors' CD for Reed's Cognition: Theory and applications* (6th ed.). Pacific Grove, CA: Wadsworth.

Reschly, A., Huebner, E., Appleton, J., & Antaramian, S. (2008). Engagement as flourishing: The contribution of positive emotions and coping to adolescents' engagement at school and with learning. *Psychology in the Schools, 45*, 419–431.

Ritchhart, R., Church, M., & Morrison, K. (2011). *Making thinking visible. How to promote engagement, understanding, and independence for all learners.* San Francisco, CA: Jossey-Bass.

Roediger, H. L., & Karpicke, J. D. (2006). Test-enhanced learning: Taking memory tests improves long-term retention. *Psychological Science, 17*, 249–255.

Rosenshine, B., & Berliner, D. C. (1978). Academic engaged time. *British Journal of Teacher Education, 4*, 3–16.

Runco, M. A., & Acar, S. (2012). Divergent thinking as an indicator of creative potential. *Creativity Research Journal, 24*(1), 66–75.

Samson, G. E., Graue, M. E., Weinstein, T., & Walberg, H. J. (1984). Academic and occupational performance: A quantitative synthesis. *American Educational Research Journal, 21*(2), 311–321.

Schneider, W. (1993). Domain-specific knowledge and memory performance in children. *Educational Psychology Review, 5*, 257–273.

Schuler, H., Funke, U., & Baron-Boldt, J. (1990). Predictive validity of school grades: A meta-analysis. *Applied Psychology: An International Review, 39*(1), 89–103.

Schunk, D., & Zimmerman, B. (2003). Self-regulation and learning. In W. Reynolds & G. Miller (Eds.), *Handbook of psychology: Vol. 7. Educational psychology* (pp. 59–78). New York, NY: Wiley.

Skinner, E., Kinderman, T., & Furrer, C. (2009). A motivational perspective on engagement and disaffection: Conceptualization and assessment of children's behavioral and emotional participation in academic activities in the classroom. *Educational and Psychological Measurement, 69*, 493–525.

Sousa, D. A. (2011). *How the brain learns* (4th ed.). Thousand Oaks, CA: Corwin.

Spires, H. A., & Donley, J. (1998). Prior knowledge activation: Inducing engagement with informational texts. *Journal of Educational Psychology, 90*(2), 249–260.

Squire, L. R. (2004). Memory systems of the brain: A brief history and current perspective. *Neurobiology of Learning and Memory, 82*, 171–177.

Stensvold, M. S., & Wilson, J. T. (1990). The interaction of verbal ability with concept mapping in learning from a chemistry laboratory activity. *Science Education, 74*, 473–480.

Timperely, H., Wilson, A., Barrar, H., & Fung, H. (2007). *Teacher professional learning and development. Best evidence synthesis iteration [BES].* Wellington, New Zealand: Ministry of Education.

Tobias, S. (1994). Interest, prior knowledge, and learning. *Review of Educational Research, 64* (1), 37–54.

Vrugt, A., & Oort, F. (2008). Metacognition, achievement goals, study strategies, and academic achievement: Pathways to achievement. *Metacognition and Learning, 3*, 123–146.

Wang, Z., Bergin, C., & Bergin, D. A. (2014). Measuring engagement in fourth to twelfth grade classrooms: The classroom engagement inventory. *School Psychology Quarterly, 29*(4), 517–535.

Willingham, D. T. (2009). *Why don't students like school? A cognitive scientist answers questions about how the mind works and what it means for the classroom.* San Francisco, CA: Jossey-Bass.

Willingham, W., & Daniel, D. B. (2012). Beyond differentiation: Teaching to what learners have in common. *Educational Leadership, 69*(5), 16–21.

Winn, W. (1991). Learning from maps and diagrams. *Educational Psychology Review, 3*, 211–247.

Yair, G. (2000). Educational battlefields in America: The tug-of-war over students' engagement with instruction. *Sociology of Education, 73*(4), 247–269.

Yan, V. X., Clark, C. M., & Bjork, R. A. (2017). Memory and metamemory considerations in the instruction of human beings revisited. In J. C. Horvath, J. M. Lodge, & J. Hattie (Eds), *From the laboratory to the classroom. Translating science of learning for teachers* (pp. 61–78). New York, NY: Routledge.

Zembal-Saul, C., McNeill, K. L., & Hershberger, K. (2012). *What's your evidence?: Engaging K–5 children in constructing explanations in science.* Boston, MA: Pearson.

Index